THE ART
OF
MANAGING
HUMANS

Management Practices
that Actually Work

TSVIKA ABRAMOVITCH

Producer & International Distributor
eBookPro Publishing
www.ebook-pro.com

THE ART OF MANAGING HUMANS
Tsvika Abramovitch

Contact: tsvikabr@pelephone.co.il

ISBN 9798871413692

This book is dedicated, with love,
to my wife Mickey (Michal)
for her support and her companionship
throughout my whole career
and to my wonderful children

"Love is not just looking at each other,
it's looking in the same direction"

Antoine de Saint-Exupéry

CONTENTS

Introduction 7

**CHAPTER 1: The Practicalities of
the Work-Related World**

The Way we Were, The Way we Are! 19

HR: A History 28

The Incarnation of a Concept: LOYALTY 36

VPs of HR How should they be Measured? 42

Coronavirus Time for a Revolution....................................53

The Effect of Coronavirus on Our Organizations............. 62

**CHAPTER 2: Assessment and Mapping
Inspired by the *Seesaw Model***

The Seesaw Model – Six Stages 78

**CHAPTER 3: Mapping the Strengthsand
Weaknesses – It is Not All Theory!**

(The Three Initial Stages of the Model)

Personal Discussions Not All at Once! 90

Roundtable Discussions Take Note! 100

'Freestyle Field Trips' Discussions from the Field.......... 104

A Model that Makes Senseand Aims
Straightfor the Heart 106

Styles of Management – How is the Chain Connected?
(The Third Stage of the Model – Analysis) 117

Outdoor Events Smart Games
(The Fourth Stage of the Model) 124

**CHAPTER 4: The Seesaw of Organizational
Powers Assessment Follow-UpProcesses**
(The Fifth Stage of the Model)

Prejudice Have You Checked Down Below as Well?........144

We Found a Junior Worker in Napoleon's Knapsack......147

Managers, Employees and In-Betweens...........................159

Human Capital A Fruitful Investment
(The Sixth Stage of the Model) 164

'Everyone Is Human Resources'
So Double the Effort! 172

**CHAPTER 5: Tomorrow, Starting Today –
Who Will the Next CEO Be?**

From Computer Engineering to Jazz 199

A Little Selfishness Can Help 213

A Point to Consider – Who Should Really Be
Entitled to Manage?..219

My Compass – From Working Relationships
to Relationships that Work.. 223

Refrences.. 224

INTRODUCTION

*"In the end, all business operations can be
reduced to three words: people, product, and profits.
People come first. Unless you've got a good team,
you can't do much with the other two"*

Lee Iacocca

I already know exactly the way the conversation will transpire. A friend or colleague or maybe a family member will ask, "Wow, Zvika! Did you really write a book? No way! How did that happen?"

Once again, I will be obliged to tell how everything unfolded...

So, it actually all began while I was having a conversation with a friend who has worked in the field for many years, who knows me and my résumé, very well. We were in the midst of professional and personal small talk, when he said, "Listen, you have done, you have been, and you have conquered. Why don't you write an article or something else telling people about your journey and your experiences? It could be of great public service to others."

In the beginning, the idea seemed far-fetched. What exactly could I accomplish by publishing something professional yet theoretical?

However, slowly but surely, I found myself thinking seriously about the matter. I began to consolidate data, eventually sitting down and writing an article where I likened employee-management relations to the endless movement of a seesaw.

I distributed the article among friends, academics, CEOs and HR managers and to my great surprise, I received positive feedback.

One of those who responded was a professor at the *Technion*.[1] He was a consultant for the organization where I was working at the time.

He said to me, and I quote from memory, "What is really unique here is that you did the opposite. First, you were in the field and then you wrote an article. You did not create a theory, as we do in academia, and then try to apply it. This order of things makes the insight different –more feasible."

After publishing the article in Israel – that same friend who had pushed me to write it – urged me forward into what he called 'stage two', meaning submitting the article to competitions around the world. As usual, my immediate reaction was, "Why? What good will it do?"

His reply was that the exposure would benefit both my potential readers and myself. Then, under his breath, he added, "After that you'll write a book."

After much self-deliberation, I reached a decision

---

1. Technion - Israel Institute of Technology

and submitted the article to global competitions. Once again, I was pleasantly surprised – the article won a few international prizes.

These prizes were awarded to me in 2012 and 2014. The gap of eight years between that discussion and the book debuting is an indication of the time it took me to reach this decision.

The Seesaw Model:
Relationships in Search of Balance

The idea on which that article was written is indeed the guideline to this book as well. I called it *The Seesaw Model* – and not by coincidence.

I developed the model with the understanding that creating a stable and fruitful relationship between employees and management is the central axis around which virtually everything in organizations takes place. Manager and employee relationships are the center gravity that dictates in which direction the company is headed – success or failure, profitability or loss, growth or stagnation.

The idea of the seesaw stemmed from the above understanding, and it professes to proclaim something simple – working relationships are not something that survive on their own. If you allow relationships to simply unfold, without any thought or planning, you will end up having to resolve endless disputes on the spot. This will have a negative outcome for any organization. However, if you create balanced working relationships, you will be able to achieve stability that will greatly reduce crises that seemingly arise out of nowhere.

In order to balance working relationships, one needs

to invest in human capital. This investment includes many fields that we are all familiar with: employee and management development, career paths, employee welfare, open discussions, employee involvement and attentiveness, and of course transparency – the latter being the most dramatic aspect in this balance. Anything that calls attention to the employee's needs and desires in an organization, which are the factors that balance out the management side with the employee side, is in constant motion – just like on a seesaw.

There are times when one side pulls down on the working relationships more, requiring you to be vigilant and restore the balance. In other words, if a developing crisis causes pressure on the working relationships, it would be incorrect to attack the issue and deal with it specifically. If you maintain constant balance, you will notice if the balance tilts. You can find its source and act accordingly. Take for example a situation where there is a major organizational change in a company. This immediately puts everyone under stress and pressure, resulting in a decline in functionality. It is an event that, if you react to it correctly and in a timely manner, as well as invest in transparency for the employees and their involvement in the process (even if to some extent it is directed by management), it will have a great impact on restoring balance to the organization.

Usually when you talk about working relationships, it refers to the rules and regulations, the conflicts and the agreements – the legal hard topics. When I talk about working relationships, I refer to the second part of the expression as well: to the relationships in the company, the organizational culture and discourse. This is a broad field, affected by many things, which in turn, affects the results of the organization.

Precisely nowadays, when flexibility and dynamics are required in order to adapt to a world that is moving at a crazy pace – the concept of the seesaw is more essential than ever. If we are not aware of the need for constant balance, we might suddenly find ourselves in a situation where one side is completely down on the ground with the other side somewhere up in the air.

The chapters in this book are designed according to the stages of the model. All the operative tools as well as the processes and effects the seesaw model has on working relationships are detailed – everything worthwhile and necessary to add to an organization's routine. If I follow the details in the book, will I be able to stop all subsequent outbursts in the workplace? Of course not!

The seesaw, by its very nature, will continue to go up and down as long as there are forces on both sides. Crises **will** occur; however, they will be controlled and with much less intensity. Therefore, if you think about it rationally, you will understand that the daily, prolonged use of the model can save an organization a lot of money, time, and additional resources, as well as preventing a dramatic turn, which tilts the seesaw completely to one side. We all know how much energy and strength is needed to tilt it back up.

Knowledge and Experience Make Up the Tools

One of the catalysts for writing this book was the understanding that this kind of book can really help – just as

I have helped many who have worked with me over the years. What I am most proud of is that I have always managed to nurture and advance managers.

There are several managers, some even working as VPs, scattered in many companies who have worked with me, and I feel I have contributed to them professionally. Of course, they did not become managers because of me, but I assume that the fact that I always advocated the need to develop employees, to allow them to be at the forefront of the stage, did its thing. Throughout their journey, they always refer back to me saying things like, 'Thank you for the tools you gave me. I use them again and again.'

Even today, by the way, the managers continue to reach out for consultations, and it is to their credit that I attribute the fact that I am constantly receiving requests for consultations or job offers from organizations I do not even know. Here is proof that rumors can also help with promotion. It may be thanks to these rumors that, throughout my whole career, I have never had a single job interview and therefore have never actually experienced what it is really like to compete for a position. In almost every case, I was approached and offered the job. There are some disadvantages to this as well, but it is what it is!

In the following chapters, I have written about all the knowledge that I have accumulated over the years. Luckily for me, my path in the world of Human Resources (HR) began as a member of a workers' committee in a large organization. In light of this, I experienced the work situation from a different perspective, which obviously widened my professional outlook. After that, I worked in a couple of large companies where I experienced different ways of dealing with management and working environments.

In addition to my ongoing work, I acquired knowledge all the time. I studied and trained myself in any field I felt I was not able to master. This included a mediation course, court sittings, analyzing balance sheets and financial reports, as well as Human Resource analysis. I participated in trainings, took courses and seminars in Israel and around the world.

From all of the above, I learned something, eventually accumulating into a large toolbox, which I use repeatedly, even today. That is definitely a part of my professional agenda. I recommend that all employees and managers do the same – in any part of your professional field where you feel less confident, go and learn the basics. It is important to understand the actual core meaning of things.

For example, when I wanted to understand how labor courts really work, I sat through hours of legal proceedings. I would check which sessions were on a specific day and I would sit and spectate. Overall, from my observations I learnt in depth how procedures are conducted on the ground. This kind of approach enriches you, providing you with tools you never know when will come in handy.

In parallel to the above, I also served as an advisory director in an insurance and pension company – two worlds that interested me as a work tool. I volunteered to help Ethiopian students, which enabled me to appreciate social philanthropy. For quite a long time, I was also a guest speaker in a Human Resources course at Haifa University and Bar-Ilan University – a field that required organizational skills, knowledge, plus other skills and it was definitely an enriching experience.

Sleepless Nights are a Given

It is important for me to stipulate that, at the beginning of my professional career, I tried my best to accumulate knowledge and to organize it in a feasible model. After my position in the first company, I thought the model might work, but of course, I did not dare spread the idea – not even to myself. Neither after the second company. It was only after the third time that I managed to make progress, stopping to take in the fact that something may actually be accurate. It may actually work.

From the above, you can understand that a substantial part of my professional knowledge was acquired through fieldwork. There were times when I just acted from my gut – not really knowing if it was a successful step or not. On the other hand, I never acted in haste. I would test myself over and over, checking one more time – though, until you actually do something, you cannot know what the results will be.

For example, when we worked on the *Atudot Project*, which I will elaborate on later, we decided to allow the opportunity for 60 employees in an organization of thousands to be promoted to management positions. We received many responses to our decision, most of them stating that this decision will only cause disappointment and bitterness among the employees.

Eventually, 500 employees applied for the promotion, of which 60 were accepted. There was not a single complaint. Of course, during this time, as during many others, I had my fair share of sleepless nights. It is important to remember that when you lead in your footsteps, especially big ones, your insides will tremble. It is all part of the game!

Not only have I worked in different companies and held many positions in my long professional life, but naturally, I have also experienced dramatic changes in organizational processes. This is why the first chapter of this book is dedicated to the dramatic shocks that have occurred in the work-related world over the years. Looking back, it is hard to grasp how employee-manager relationships have changed over a few decades.

As if these shocks were not enough, Coronavirus came and shuffled all the cards. Therefore, when reviewing the work-related world in the past and in the future, it is impossible not to dedicate a whole section only for the Coronavirus – a kind of unforeseen circle of review.

The Bottom Line: I Hope I will be an Open Book for You

In my view, the relationships between managers and employees, taking into account everything in between, are business tools – just like any others. However, unfortunately, even today, I do not think this attitude is a contemporary one in the field.

We all know how to recite in general terms that the worker is the most precious resource in a company, but the question is – what is actually being done with this understanding. The advantage of all that I have written here is that these are not theoretical declarations that sound good, but descriptions of facts, processes, and results in the field.

The actual process and order of things I describe are backed by stories of events that actually happened to me during my career. Decades of work have called for many of them, and I hope that I manage to convey my point of view in its entirety.

In order to keep up with the innovations in the global world of HR, I have also read many management books throughout the years, which have helped me write this particularly practical book. Therefore, due to its practicality, I hope readers will not only connect and relate with what is written, but will also adopt and apply the model – each in their own little world.

From my point of view, the best accomplishment of this book will be for managers to have it on hand, open on their desks, and not on the shelf with their other business books. Even if one reader reports that they acted according to the book and it was successful, or another would say that the book made some feasible order out of things they already knew – I would feel that I have succeeded in my quest.

I really hope that for you, my readers, this book will become a permanent work tool. I believe that if I had read this book when I started my career in HR, it would have shortened some processes and paved my way much quicker to areas of success. I am confident that there are a few people who this book will help do just that!

CHAPTER 1

The Practicalities of the
Work-Related World

THE WAY WE WERE,
THE WAY WE ARE!

*"Change will not come if we wait for
some other person or some other time.
We are the ones we've been waiting for.
We are the change that we seek"*

Barack Obama

In one of the unforgettable scenes from the movie *Revolutionary Road* that takes place in the 50's, you see the hero (Leonardo DiCaprio) going to his mundane job, together with hundreds of other clerks. He tries passing the day with as few run-ins with his boss as possible, doing his monotonous work, with no aspirations or interest. His only wish is to bring home a salary at the end of the month and maybe receive a tiny promotion and tenure. The highlight of his day is a little office gossip, which of course circles mainly around the managers.

Given how real the scene I described is, it makes for a great opening when aiming to review the changes and upheavals that have taken place, at a relatively fast pace, in the workplace in general as well as in the field of Human Resources.

Hence, we begin the journey into the *Seesaw Model* with a revolution – to better understand what is happening in the work-related world nowadays, to understand what changes have occurred and what should happen in the future for all our sakes – employees, managers, and company owners alike.

Perception in Motion, Where is the Intellect?

Let us begin by stating that not so long ago, in my parents' generation for example, in the 1950's, 60's, 70's and maybe even the 80's, DiCaprio's work circumstances in the movie were basically the norm everywhere. You could easily find someone who had been working in the same place, doing the same job for 30 – 40 years and who was completely satisfied with it. Everyone accepted this work situation as a fact. Life was simple back then – getting a salary from an organized workplace meant success. It was quite an ingrained concept. Since there were not as many ways for society to connect, as well as a lot less exposure to knowledge, being aware of and understanding situations around you and other potential possibilities was not even part of one's agenda back then.

Today, young people are a lot more knowledgeable. The youth are exposed to many more fields of interest, directly resulting in them having less commitment to their place of work. They may be committed, but the days of total and complete loyalty are over. The prevailing attitude is that one should no longer work in the same workplace until retirement because one should aspire to move on and evolve.

Another significant point relates to the inconceivable way the balance of power used to be in the workplace. It is difficult to describe how submissive the workers were in the 50s up until the 80s. Today this would be perceived as being a pushover. Instructions were given and that was it. A counter-response was not even a thought. Management had the knowledge and made the decisions, and the managers led accordingly. The words 'managers will manage, and the workers will work' was a key sentence in many organizations for countless years.

This absolute subordination, which was born many generations back, existed everywhere and not just in the workplace. Take doctors for example – not too long ago, doctors were highly regarded as educated experts who know exactly what they are saying. But today, patients start their treatment by first Googling their symptoms and self-diagnosing, after which they look at online comparisons of experts to find who is best fit to treat their specific illness. After they finally go to the expert, they might even consider a second opinion. The challenge of authority is general and comprehensive.

That same way of thinking also made employees believe that only managers were smart – a notion that was refuted ages ago, of course. However, one should remember that the concept 'management' then was considered very amorphous. There was the 'management building' where no one but management belonged and everyone else was invisible. This situation was known and accepted by all. It was the norm back then.

If somehow, one got lucky and was promoted to manager, once that sign was on the door, it was no longer important whether they had appropriate leadership skills, knowledge, or professionalism. 'YOU are the manager!'

Nowadays authority is disputable. It is less about not being prepared to accept orders and more about having the ability to express your opinion, which may differ to your superiors. Employers have also reached the understanding that there is an advantage to harnessing multiple opinions and making them wisdom of the crowd. Therefore, there are managers today who tend to include employees in decision-making processes and dilemma solutions.

"Change is a threat when done to me, but an opportunity when done by me"

Rosabeth Moss Kanter

Having a Rich Father?
May Be Nice But it is Not a Must!

The undermining of authority, new standards of expectations and the revolution in information, have all created a completely different workplace. These changes have advantages and disadvantages for employers as well as employees. Firstly, employees move from one job to another more frequently, so recruiters' work is much more complex. They need to attract employees by creating high interest, future employment horizons, career paths and suitable company values for the employee to feel that it is not just a place of work, but also a place where they can be heard, express themselves and evolve.

These changes may have made things more difficult for managers. However, they have also brought about exposure of information, which, in my opinion, benefits us all. For example, the fact that only a small percentage of people hold most of the global wealth.

I do not remember people ever talking about management's salaries when I was a young worker. Not only was the subject taboo, but at the time, the difference in salary between employees and managers was not so extreme.

Nowadays, all the information is out there, including the astronomical salaries some managers receive. This can cause outrage, feelings of alienation and a lot less loyalty amongst employees. If employees feel they are significantly contributing to their place of employment, but their salaries are low in comparison to the managers – the same feelings will arise. These issues, causing anger and pressure at the bottom of the food chain, escalate to grievances and can even cause employees to rally together, and this needs to be taken into account by every manager. This has a great impact on the workplace.

In conjunction with all the above, there has been a revolution in the field of raising capital. In the past, if someone wanted to establish a business or a company and they did not have a rich father, their chances of raising the initial capital were almost nonexistent. Today, anyone who has an idea can build a business plan and try to find investors from crowdfunding, venture funds or even banks, which earn a lot of interest from these loans. Therefore, establishing a business nowadays with no initial equity is less problematic.

Another aspect of change is in the field of technological knowledge. In the past, companies could keep their work processes a secret. Today, you can surf the Internet and learn how to do almost anything. There are a few companies like *Coca-Cola* for example, whose secret formula is still under lock and key, but they are rare. In most cases, if you want to establish a business in any field, you are exposed to information that in the past even money could not buy.

In addition to the field of knowledge, there are changes to the field of equipment as well. In the past, it was a major deal having to buy machinery and any other industrial equipment. Options were very limited, processes were long and prices were sky high. Today, there is no problem. If you cannot find what you are looking for on the Internet, there are other places to look, including in other countries and you can always find cheaper options.

Considering all the components that were once used to give companies advantages, today you have reached the situation where there is no *a priori* priority. There are no longer any advantages. Whatever you create today, there will always be someone after you who can do it better and cheaper.

"The secret of change is to focus all of your energy not on fighting the old, but on building the new"

Socrates

Caution: (No) Border Ahead

Another aspect of change that would have caused DiCaprio's character in the movie to rub his eyes in disbelief is the topic of employees and their goals. Who would have dreamed it possible to present a business plan to employees?

Nowadays, there is dialogue even with employees at the most junior level about their goals, work plans and results. What was once a very clear and strict hierarchy, in which it was impossible to move upwards, today organizations have a much flatter work hierarchy, with a lot more knowledge going down the pyramid and sometimes even back up to the top. Of course, in order to have a much wider system, you need to invest more to maintain it.

In short, back then, managers communicated instructions to the employees. The employees followed out these instructions and that was the end of the story.

Today we are in a completely different world!

Another one of the characteristics of a flatter work hierarchy is the phenomenon of relocation. Due to global mobility, employees can be managed from any place. Borders are unclear if not non-existent. Today, you can work wherever you choose, no longer having limitations. The world is open. Employers should look to cultivate their human resources, with the awareness that the range of opportunities for employees is wider than anyone thought possible.

Naturally, what was considered important in the workplace in the past has totally changed over the years. Your salary, working conditions, accessibility and social security were most important. Now, people look for a job that has meaning, employee involvement, possibilities for promotion and evolvement. In other words, the question of what is considered 'a good place to work' is perceived by us all to be a much more complex one.

Already at this point, the necessary question arises – wherein lies an employer's competitive advantage? The logical answer is mainly in Human Resources. In the past few years, this fact has begun to sink in more deeply. The quality of employees, their motivation, wisdom, and knowledge, as well as their level of involvement and commitment – make up the ammunition with which the battle is won. Human resources have become the crucial resource – the real resource. This applies to all fields.

Take, for example, the field of sales. What matters is not what you are selling, but who is selling the product. The salesperson who is motivated and satisfied, connected to the agenda, and exposed to the organization's goals – will be the better salesperson.

The significance of all the changes described above have led us to perceive our workplace differently today. It is seen not only as a source of livelihood, but also as a place where you spend most of your time. This concept includes the need to provide challenges, meet desires and to adapt to the worldview and social agenda of the employees.

This is all well and good but let us not forget that the need for a business to be profitable has not changed. In other words, the whole matter takes on greater volume and complexity than ever before, as not only do managers need to deal with balance sheets, but they also need to deal with balancing out the working relationships. All this leads to the understanding that many investments and details are required when answering the question: What exactly does it mean to nurture an employee?

"It is impossible to estimate how many good ideas are neglected every day as a result of relationships not managed correctly"

John P. Kotter

HR:
A HISTORY

Along with the dramatic changes in the work-related world, the HR mechanism has also undergone an evolution, which, only upon taking a retrospective view, it is possible to grasp the full scope and meaning

L ooking back, not hundreds of years, but only around 30-40 years, we will find that everything began with a 'mechanism'. Clerks would write down attendance hours, prepare pay slips and employ people for the job. Getting a job did not include an interview, only filling out forms containing bureaucratic details – not a word about the essence of the person.

No one thought to get to know the candidates and interview them – learn about who they were and their aspirations. Whether these things were important or not, they were not part of the agenda. One would show up for a job interview and after a few minutes or slightly longer, be accepted for the job. After filling out the necessary forms, work begins.

In the years that followed, the mechanism started taking on a different form. There was a wider reference to the company's needs and the requirements necessary to carry out the specific job. With the mechanism in place, in most workplaces (especially in industry), it did not really matter what your skills and abilities were or whether you wanted to work as a production worker, a laborer or a clerk. You began to work and learned while going through the motions. The manpower departments slowly began to check who should be working where, but on a very small scope. Employees were still not related to as human resources, but more like a workforce or manpower. It is probably not by chance that this was the name given.

In time, 'manpower' became 'human resources', and after a long process of development, workers began to be considered human resources. As human resources, there should be a better screening and recruitment process, adapting them to the required jobs.

Slowly it became clear that there was no choice but to track the developments in the working world, a world that was becoming more and more complex. Requirements like knowledge, education and pre-training were becoming a necessity. There were certain jobs that without a certain level of education were inadmissible. The phenomenon of 'growing within', which until then had been applicable in all fields, even in the field of computers, was no longer relevant.

I remember a specific case of a junior payroll accountant, who gradually began to enter the field of computers. After a few years, from a clerk with minimum elementary school education, he became a computer systems manager at a very high level. He had the ability and time to learn, but mainly he had been given the opportunity.

More the Business, Less the Persona!

The transformation in the field of HR did not happen overnight. It was a development that took many years.

Following the initial focus of recruiting and screening, HR slowly began to develop. It began slowly with trainings and courses that were very goal-oriented and specific. It was more about what the business needed and less about the persona – the worker. Everything was done in a very clear, square framework. There was more human resources training, and fewer human resources development.

In time, when jobs began to require workers with more initiative, more involvement and broader thinking, the world began to shift in the real direction of developing employees individually. This trend of organizational development grew, especially in the USA, while in Israel – everyone tried keeping up.

This was definitely a different way of thinking. It related to the needs of the workplace as an organization and raised the question of how we, as human resources, can contribute to the business goals of the company. At that stage, the changes were still being maintained on a minimal level.

In recent decades, buds of career paths have sprouted up and the issue of employees moving around from within the system has gained momentum. It was no longer about remaining in a job until retirement.

As a side note, it is worth stating that it is difficult to perceive the rigid ceilings that were created as a result of the norm back then – which was to leave a job only for retirement. These are ceilings that blocked any development, leaving no room for change. It was not an easy task to break through the veterans' way of knowing and thinking with these innovations and different outlooks.

There were barriers of all kinds that were not challenged, but accepted and the employees worked under these conditions, performing as best as they could within these frameworks. That was the first stage of the beginning of the formation of HR– as we know it today. At this stage, HR was included in positions of management, but not as key, influential players. The understanding that the greatest resource is manpower, brought on the realization that HR is a necessity, not from a leadership aspect, but more in the way of serving the needs of the workplace.

"Either I will find a way, or I will make one"
Philip Sidney

We are still Chasing after Yesterday's Problems!

In the next relatively advanced stage, HR was perceived as a business partner. Although this was required to bring added value to a business, it had not yet been perceived as responsible for leading changes, for the organizational culture, or for recruiting the most suitable employees, training them and their development. All of these developed along with the competition in the job market. Employees moved from workplace to workplace, receiving several offers at the same time and very quickly, the job market became more dynamic, rocking companies' thresholds. New challenges had to be faced!

Of course, this caused other repercussions. For example, I remember that when the mechanism and manpower were in place, and even at the beginning of HR as we know it today, there was never a problem recruiting an employee. Once a job had been advertised, there would be candidates. Simple as can be! Nowadays, recruitment is extremely difficult, since several companies compete for the same resource. They all want the best. The competition is substantial on all fronts.

Technology obviously has a huge impact on this development. The generation has changed together with their frame of mind. Situations are no longer just accepted and performed – with no second-guessing. Back in the day, people of my generation still remember that a father's authority was hardly ever undermined. In other words, even the basis of parental authority has completely changed over the years. A substantial part of it has to do with the gaining of knowledge.

We would get our knowledge from our parents because they had basically been our only source of information at the time. There were encyclopedias and public libraries, but that was it. Today, thanks to the exposure and availability of knowledge, children think they know it all, and the truth is that there are definitely things about which they are better informed than we adults are.

Everything mentioned above created a change not only in the perception of the internal family hierarchy, but also in the world in general and obviously in the business world specifically. Today, young employees are more knowledgeable, at least in certain fields, taking nothing for granted. There is no such thing as a higher authority. The question 'Can it maybe be done differently?' is always an option.

The changes in technology and the formation of the young, opinionated employee automatically affected the development of human resources. HR needed to create a new world that had never been lived in – a world where the competition for human resources was unprecedented. Once employees started relocating to other companies, the competition began.

Looking at the contemporary place of HR, it has become the business partner – looking at the human capital from a business aspect.

Now, the next stage is on the cards – a stage where human resources will actually lead the changes and goals in the organization. It is obvious that behind it all – engineering, technology, marketing and sales – you will find the people running them!

As someone responsible for the human capital, one needs to make sure that the best answer is found in all the above fields. It was once believed that bringing on a good engineer would solve all engineering problems. Today it is obvious that is not the case! It is important to understand how involved and influenced the engineer is feeling, because tomorrow morning he might resign. There is nothing to stop anyone; neither pressure from family nor social pressures that once were a dominant influence for staying in an 'organized' workplace.

Surprise, Surprise!
The Outburst is Already Here!

With regards to 'organized' workplaces – I cannot help but mention the dream that all Jewish mothers had for their sons while I was growing up in Haifa, a city in

Northern Israel. They all wanted their sons to work in the local bus company. Who would have thought?

As I mentioned before, even though the field of HR has developed, it is still in a place where the solutions provided only solve yesterday's problems. It is true that one of the factors that slowed down the growth in the field, in the face of its developing needs, was that managements did not fully grasp the implications of the changes, even if they understood the process at hand. They maintained things at the level of 'Yes, change should happen, but it is not the highest priority, it can be ignored.' We did not see the whole picture. We only saw what was on the surface. What was invisible began to move at such a tremendous pace – we only saw it when the outburst had already occurred.

If we had recognized the underground currents at the start, we might have been able to save ourselves many crises and misunderstandings. If we had recognized and been alerted beforehand, managements and boards of directors might have perceived the importance of HR, positioning them in a better place.

Let us admit it – I know many managers who lose sleep over sales, performances, financial situations, and market competition. I do not know many managers who have sleepless nights because HR have neglected employee development. It is not something that any manager loses sleep over.

When **do** you start losing sleep? When crises happen. Obviously, it is more conspicuous in places where workers are organized – but not only there. On the continuum, there are also cases where seemingly reliable employees would come to work in the morning, do nothing and then leave in the afternoon – and management was unaware.

It is likely that if they had provided the right processes for these employees – structured processes in HR – of which today we know how to translate into practicalities, the situation would have looked different. If maybe the employees had been spoken to, allowing their needs to be recognized and given the opportunity to voice their opinions, a large part of hidden unemployment and turnover could have been avoided. And then, yes, we might all have been caught less by surprise!

It goes without saying that in organized workplaces, the progressions are more visible, because the incorrect mapping and handling are manifested in the general working relationships, which only make things worse. It is not just one solitary case that can be swallowed and dealt with.

If we are looking at things retrospectively, the general trend in past years, as most of us are aware, is employees' organizations sprouting up at an alarming rate. Who would have ever thought we would be talking about such a thing? To a certain extent, this is also happening because of the information revolution. There is great exposure and transparency of information. Everyone knows and can see what is happening all over the world bringing on questions like, 'Hold on a minute! Why are things not like that with us? Really! How come?'

> *"Loyalty that is bought with money –*
> *may be overcome by money"*
> **Seneca**

THE INCARNATION OF A CONCEPT:
LOYALTY

The summary of the work-related world and of HR brought here, raise certain questions that resonate with many managers of employees. One of the more interesting questions is regarding the concept of loyalty in the workplace – is there still such a thing?

In my opinion, loyalty is still around but the shape has changed. There is no point in searching for and judging loyalty in years gone past, because nowadays, for you to be a loyal employee, many more things need to exist. The days when having a salary and good employment conditions automatically bought your loyalty are over!

In the past, being a loyal employee mainly meant staying at your job. In its present manifestation, loyalty means something else. Obviously, there are employees who, to a large extent, identify with their workplace, but it is more like 'I am loyal as long as I work here, but not at any cost. I am always aware that there are other options.'

It is more precise maybe to distinguish between loyalty and a certain kind of commitment, because today it is much easier for employees to move from place to place. In the past, these were major dilemmas. Now, not only is it much easier to leave a job, it is considered part of the norm. For the sake of exaggeration, we can even say that up until a few years ago, leaving your job was considered a betrayal of the place that nurtured you and provided for you.

Today the situation is almost completely reversed – part of the employee's perception is that employers should be grateful for their employees. There is a lot more awareness among employees regarding their contribution. Even though some may still think that they are only a small link in the chain, they are more aware of their contribution; they share their knowledge and their abilities and are therefore a part of the company's success. In the past, one never heard of this.

Therefore, today it is more complicated to create a feeling of loyalty in employees because it entails many elements. Overall, in order for employees to be loyal, or even just do their best at work, they need to feel a part of something bigger. They need to feel that their opinions count, that they are informed about the goings-on and that the information they receive is relevant.

Another issue to take into consideration is the impact of the chain of management on the degree of loyalty. Of course, it begins with the CEO – their style of management and their reference to the employees and the organizational culture. However, in my opinion, this has a small effect. The lower down the ladder we go and the closer we get to the direct manager, the more effect there is on whether employees feel connected and committed to the organization. A huge factor on how employees feel towards their workplace has to do with how much they feel their opinions are respected and whether they are seen and heard on a regular basis. Of course, the example their direct managers show has great importance, because they are usually more visible and accessible than the other managers.

Incentives for Managers, Who left Who?

One of the more interesting examples of this impact came across my path recently. It began with the problem we are facing, like everyone else in the market, with the recruitment for call centers. It is a serious problem – a difficult one to overcome.

After an in-depth analysis, we found that generally, after three months of employment, about 50 percent of all call center employees leave. A crazy turnover! Not that it is of any comfort, but the situation is the same for anyone running a call center.

We began an in-depth study of the reasons for employee departures, and mapped out in which call centers it happens and what the percentages are. We located the call centers with the highest turnover rate, and, on the other end, we located call centers in which the employees stay for much longer periods of time. Obviously, we located the whole range – borderline and average, but we focused mainly on places where the turnover was extreme – some cases even an 80 percent turnover. We decided to look into who the managers were. We interviewed a few employees and checked with the managers of their managers, and it turned out that the decisive effect was the direct manager.

Even we were surprised by the extreme responses we received. When asking employees why they were satisfied at their workplace, long-term employees answered in terms of, 'I like coming here. When I come in the morning, I am treated nicely. My manager shows an interest in how I am doing, sometimes even working next to me to see if I need any assistance. I feel comfortable asking my coworkers or even my manager when I am faced with a challenge.'

Even when widening the circle to include veteran employees, we found a difference in the general atmosphere in the call center, compared to call centers where employee turnover is high. In other words, direct managers have a huge impact.

As a result of this analysis, we introduced measurable parameters for reducing employee abandonment in the manager's incentive models. In other words, managers are required not only to perform, but will also be rewarded if they meet their goals. Since these positions depend on incentives versus performance, it became clear that employee turnover had to be a significant factor when evaluating the managers, together with their incentives. Although we are only in the beginning of these processes, we can already see buds of transformation and a trend of improvement.

Therefore, what is derived from the above is that one of the factors connecting employees to their workplace and enhancing their loyalty is their manager's personal example. You cannot sell slogans, when in reality they are not actually implemented. If senior managers do not work toward their professed goals, this undoubtedly permeates downwards, affecting their employees' behavior and choices.

In general, I feel that management today, especially the management of large groups of employees, has transformed from what it initially stood for and has become leadership and role models. It is no longer about a manager sitting in a secluded office alone. Today there are meetings, discussions, decision-making processes etc. It is much broader than passing instructions down the ladder. Therefore, the ability to act as a manager, behaving admirable, as an equal with sincere empathy, has great impact.

Nowadays, there are many examples of smart and professional managers sincerely lacking in social skills. From my experience, emotional intelligence can make or break you. There are no two ways about it. It does not matter how good you are in your field. Managers today are a lot more exposed and employees' expectations from them are more focused and attentive. Employees will not follow you at any cost. I do not want to give examples of extreme and insulting cases. Let us just say that in best-case scenarios, employees will simply not be with you.

Obviously, leadership qualities and emotional intelligence directly relate to feelings of loyalty. If managers do not relate to their employees' additional circles of need, the employees' loyalty will undeniably decrease. Companies, in which employees are emotionally connected, have stronger feelings of commitment. This is especially noticeable when malfunctions or challenges occur. This is the true test!

What was once called loyalty and was interpreted as employees stagnating, staying in their jobs with blind acceptance of orders, has changed, as stated. The period of blind and complete acceptance of instructions has vanished from our world; hence, management has undergone fundamental changes, from patterns of commanding to patterns of guidance and leadership.

"Tell me and I forget. Teach me and I remember. Involve me and I learn"

Benjamin Franklin

VPs of HR
How should they be Measured?

Seeing as the positioning of HR is becoming more and more of a crucial factor, the question to be asked is who should be chosen as a VP in such a field. Who is really suitable and why is the persona especially important?

It is true that in every profession the person behind the job is important. When you employ a financial worker, that worker becomes the financial authority. The employee knows exactly what the job entails; their goals and objectives are clear, and their performance can be measured, quantified, and tracked to determine how well the job is being done.

In the field of HR, measurements are more long-term related. These are not always fields that can actually be grasped. For example, organizational culture is not something that can be quantified. It is true that you can conduct an annual survey to get a better understanding of the organization's pulse, but it is still not something that can easily be measured, as culture is more a matter of individual feelings, awareness, understanding and interpretation of those concerned.

Therefore, there is a wide range of error. Some organizations appear to be so perfect, but the top layer is all icing and underneath the cake is rotten. This happens a lot because the most common mistake managers make, even those in HR, is to look at what is happening on the surface – the obvious things that are easily located. However, these things do not always represent reality and it is only when there is a true test, does one find out what is bubbling below.

Because of the above, there is much more weight given to the persona of managers in HR: how they express themselves, their background, what management skills they have, their ability to advise and direct other managers and how well their messages are received.

As we noted earlier, the world is in a place today where HR should be leading the changes in the field of organizational culture and development and even in the most business-related fields. It was expected that these fields would get a significant boost and there would be very specific demands from whoever is in charge. This has not yet occurred!

It is possible that because HR professions entail more emotional elements, there is a balance necessary between the ability to activate these elements and the managerial skills required to harness, direct and lead people. This balance does not always exist.

Worth Checking Out, What is in Your Package?

If we look at what is usually the personal development track of a manager in HR, we will find that it is not a regular path to management. Employees can become managers by making their way up from a junior position in HR, with the relevant education, trainings and experience they have accumulated. However, a closer look reveals that on their way up to becoming VPs, they only managed the HR team, then the HR department and then the division. In other words, one bright morning, they find themselves leaders! It is not exactly the promotional track of managers in other fields, and certainly not of VPs.

The above is actually in complete contrast to what is required of a VP in HR, especially in large companies where the VP is the CEO's main advisor also in matters of management; however, the VP does not always have those capabilities. In other words, there is a built-in gap between what is expected of a VP in HR and what occurs in reality.

By the way, I have found this phenomenon relevant when dealing with external consultants as well. As someone wanting to advise senior managers, when asked who they have actually managed, I find many external consultants who have never actually been managers. They are familiar with the management field from academia, from observing and accompanying managers, but not from their own experiences of managing employees. In my opinion, there is a problem here that HR will need to address – how to create a promotion path in HR, so that before reaching the most senior levels, candidates will have had real management experience.

At the end of the day, the skills required of a manager are non-theoretical. Therefore, even if you have mastered the theory, I do not think you can properly act as VP without having actual management experience.

It seems a bit pretentious to be in a position of VP of HR without ever having managed any real conflicts. It is unreliable as a manager in HR to tell a CEO how to manage a process, when the former themselves have not had firsthand experience. No advice can be given from a textbook or from one's own personal understanding of situations. The bottom line is that the saying – *You cannot really understand another person's experience until you have walked a mile in their shoes* is very accurate here.

Lack of management experience can sometimes have major effects. Let us say that you are looking to hire someone in HR and there is an amazing candidate with the knowledge, abilities and understanding of the profession. On the surface, they may be suitable, but a closer look at their résumé shows that the candidate was a VP in a start-up of 40 employees. The position on hand is to become VP of HR in a company with thousands of employees and hundreds of managers. How prepared can they actually be?

This is the rationale for which I would highly recommend managers in HR to take on positions from other worlds as well – to gain experience in managerial performance roles as an integral part of their career development. This will substantially expand their practical understanding of management and will contribute more than any additional training taken in the field of HR itself.

"Experience is a hard teacher because she gives the test first, the lesson afterwards"
Vernon Sanders Law

Houston, We Have a Problem,
Knowledge Could Have Prevented!

There are examples of cases where an insufficient professional track in the field can cause malfunctions. For example, I was witness to an activity that we did as part of a roundtable discussion. An HR manager approached a division manager and asked him if he wanted to join a roundtable discussion with his employees, even though the HR manager himself had not had any experience with roundtable discussions. Without any warning, the discussion turned into a frontal attack on the division manager, who backed away and did not know how to respond.

It turned out that the HR manager had not properly prepared the division manager because the former himself did not fully understand the process. If he had experience, he would have familiarized himself with the division manager to understand if the latter was able to handle the situation. In fact, if he had experience in roundtable discussions, not only would the incident have been avoided, but also the division manager would have known how to handle the situation.

We know, for example, that in roundtable discussions things can get heated very quickly and turn into personal attacks. It all depends on the momentum: the timing of the discussion, how to present it and how to lead it. It is also important to remember that a reaction elicits a response and can be swept up into a vortex. Anyone experienced in these discussions knows that boundaries need to be set. It is part of managing such a process. Responses like – 'Sorry, but this is neither the time nor the place' or 'That is not what we meant' are legitimate.

It is permissible to ask to focus on specific topics and if someone has a personal issue to discuss, let them know that their manager's door is always open. There is a solution to such scenarios.

Let us look at another case study. As HR manager, you need to guide managers on how to conduct personal discussions with employees – a seemingly simple matter. Yet, it all depends on how much experience you have had to be able to provide managers with the scenarios that best suit them personally. There are many managers with different styles of management. If managers are rigid, then they need tips on how to soften up. If managers are perceived as blunt or assertive – the HR manager should know how to reflect that to them. Simulations should be conducted so that managers are aware of the different possible scenarios and how they should be handled.

HR managers usually have a wide range of knowledge in these fields, but in my opinion, they lack the personal firsthand experience, because, in the end, we are talking about human beings – it is not an exact science!

A Closed-Down Factory Is Not a Pretty Sight!

Of course, with all sensitivity, we are showing here that HR management is not a piece of cake – with infinite kindness. Far from it! As HR managers, we know how to set boundaries, to fight to the bitter end and take on complex battles.

Below is an example of where force was applied moderately and reasonably, in a way that was planned and powerful, but not forceful.

One of the companies I was working in had reached the stage of almost collapsing. For many years, the company had been a monopoly in its field and therefore was very profitable. One of the implications of the above was that a strong and militant workers' committee had been formed. As long as the company was able to, it paid all its dues and the astronomical work agreements were on autopilot, eventually bringing the company to a place where junior employees were earning salaries equivalent to deputy VPs – an absurd situation!

Management discussions began in which there were talks about salary cuts at the lower levels. As the HR manager, I told management that if there were going to be salary cuts, they need to start with the management level. Everyone turned their noses up at me, but I repeated what I believe in – you cannot make such a move without showing personal examples. It is impossible to fight a battle, as right as it may be, only on someone else's expense.

And so – we all took salary cuts.

At the same time, we approached the committee and conflicts and struggles immediately began. At some point, they imposed sanctions, the first being not to allow trucks entrance to load merchandise. They took control of the gate, which caused immense damage. Our people came to inform us that the gate to the factory had been closed.

Everyone expected that as management, and especially me, we would respond by bringing in legal assistance and getting injunctions, forcing them to open the gates. I, on the other hand, only asked if we had a large lock. When asked why, I responded that it was time to lock the gate and not open it again.

Obviously, the CEO and I were in coordination. It was clearly a difficult time for him as, at the end of the day, he was the one at the forefront. Backed by the chairperson, we closed down the factory. The employees did not understand what was going on. In Israel, there have been isolated cases of defensive lockouts, but this was not one of them.

We took the reins, which led to the closing of the factory. The *Histadrut* (the General Organization of Workers in Israel) and the committee subpoenaed us – management – to the Labor Courts, to compel us to re-open the factory. When we arrived to the hearing, the presiding judge summoned us to his chambers and told us to re-open the factory. Our response was that, if we cannot control trucks entering and leaving, or which machine is working and which is disabled, then we cannot take responsibility. The risks are too high. Either the workers work, or they do not, and if they do not, then the factory remains closed!

When the judge asked when we will re-open, we replied by saying that we will not be re-opening; we were closing down. Naturally, this move was accompanied by power struggles. We even needed to be accompanied by Border Control and SWAT Teams. A great movie with all the effects!

One morning, I arrived at the factory with the CEO. There were hundreds of employees at the entrance swarming and banging on the car, shouting loudly and displaying signboards. We got out of the car and told them that if they would like to talk, they had a committee and we would be in our office waiting. We knew it would not be long before the committee members would show up.

We convened the entire management, with the managers raising their voices, saying that we should show the employees who is boss and let them know the full force of our hand. I told them, "You are not thinking straight. When the strike ends, we will need to work with these people again. Do not hate the people you manage, because that will make work almost impossible. We are strong enough, determined enough and our message has gone through loud and clear."

After that stormy morning, one of the VPs approached me and said, "You know, I could not have said what you said if they had blocked my entry, shouted at me and cursed me, while waiving signboards at me." That is the whole point! This kind of event should not be turned into a personal fight filled with volatile emotions. It is true that we are all just human, and within such a process, we get angry and upset, but our job as managers is to constantly convey a message of determination – we believe in our way. Everything should be out in the open and so, although the employees were angry with us, at the end of the day they appreciated us as well.

"Decency renders all things tolerable"
Joseph Marie

The Law of Transparency Works for You

Here is another example of a struggle. In one of the companies I worked, we merged and joined a company that specialized in production, not in a specific region. Our branches in every city handled everything, so we merged with a company that specialized only in production. In this new process, we had to downsize many of our sites. We closed the branches in Haifa (Northern Israel), in Tel Aviv and in Jerusalem. We also centralized our distribution centers into three areas instead of seven. We took all these actions without applying force and worked with the workers' committees to provide retirement agreements for all the workers we could not place in the company. In addition, we organized structured job search procedures for employees who would be fired, including helping them write a résumé as well as initiating a job fair, bringing potential employers from the field.

The process was quite moving. An extreme example was in one of the branches, in a region known for its lack of employment, where we had to let almost all our employees go. We did whatever was needed in a very embracing and tolerant way, accommodating the employees as best as we could. At the farewell party, the workers thanked management for the process. Employees who had lost their source of livelihood said, "With all the pain in the matter, we thank you for the way you have treated us and for your patience. We highly appreciate it." It was quite unbelievable because you would expect that someone who has just lost their livelihood would tell us to take our procedures and go to hell – because starting tomorrow they would be out of a job!

In my opinion, the reason things developed the way they did, was that from the beginning and throughout the whole process, we were completely transparent with the employees. We never cheated or hid anything from them, just presented them with the full truth – even when it was a hard truth!

Obviously, I have many smaller and more trivial examples showing how mutual appreciation can work in one's favor. In one company, for example, when an employee acted inappropriately, I did not need to conduct a disciplinary inquiry or suspend them etc. I turned to the chairperson of the committee, and they worked things out with the employee. Our relationship was one of mutual respect. They knew that if I told them an employee acted wrongfully, they would automatically sort it out. Why? Because even in cases where a manager complained about an employee, and it turned out that the manager had acted wrongfully, we came out and said it. Fairness is respected even when it is not easy or does not serve one's best interest at that moment.

At the end of the day, fairness has a strong impact!

*"Not only did I break the rules I learned –
I broke rules I never even knew existed"*

Martin Scorsese

Coronavirus
Time for a Revolution

From the distant past of the work-related world to its present and future – in other words – Coronavirus!

I think we can all agree on one fact about Coronavirus – that it is still difficult to estimate the changes it has brought on. Some claim that it is all about the acceleration of processes. I belong to the school believing that the implications of Coronavirus are no less than a revolution.

Another fact regarding the virus, one that is mentioned much less, is the formation of new working relations, with the emphasis on 'relations'. I will elaborate more on this below.

The topic of working from a distance has been on the table for many years, especially due to many international companies that maintain operations worldwide. For example, in the field of call centers: a company's HQ can be in the USA while its call center is in India, even though the employees of the call center are centralized in one place and do not work from home. People in the field of programming, system administrators etc., also work from home, although on a rather smaller scale. It is true that these are cases of employees and management working from branches spread around the world and not of the mass of employees working from home. Where Coronavirus is concerned, it is a much more complicated management process.

Until today, besides just talking about it, most of us were afraid to really bring up the subject of working from home. Until the pandemic, trial runs and tests may have been conducted on a small scale, within the margins. However, suddenly, with no warning or intent and on an unimaginable scale, the whole world was thrown into the biggest 'working from home' experiment. Companies were thrown into the deep end. However, if we isolate that particular point, we may see that most organizations carried on functioning – more or less. From our experience after checking three large companies, we found that their results and outputs were satisfactory.

Are there still more questions and dilemmas rather than answers regarding this issue?

Of course there are! We are just getting started. What we had pushed to the side and labeled under 'We'll have to check it out at some point', turned out to having great advantages albeit alongside considerable difficulties. The upsides for the companies are mainly financial. The downsides and big challenges are more of what I call in the realm of 'organizational distancing' (which is a direct continuation of 'social distancing').

"Confront the difficult while it is still easy"

Lao Tzu

Connecting Through a Screen

In the 'great Coronavirus experiment', we took employees who were used to going into work, to the same place every day and connecting with the company, the discourse, the brand, the culture, and the social scene – everything that is considered the organizational vibe – and we sent them to work from home with all that baggage. Tomorrow, when we recruit someone who, from the beginning, is supposed to work from home, he or she will not have that foundation. So, how do we connect them to the organizational culture?

There are some serious problems to be dealt with and, in my view, the model presented here, aimed at creating balance in working relationships, with all its procedures, clauses and aspects will be more effective and substantial than ever – especially in times like these. Of course, there will be greater difficulties in execution, and we will need to find the tools and make adjustments, but in principle, it is the same core.

Today's existing technologies will most definitely make the adjustments easier, but many issues will require more support from HR. Take for example the already mentioned roundtable discussions (a working model in which managers and employees meet formally in a physical space, and which I will elaborate on further) – a tool to which I attach immense importance. Until today, managers would come to the roundtable discussions after meeting their employees regularly in the hallway, the coffee corner or dining room. These casual meets provide a lot of informal information.

Therefore, it was sufficient to have formal group meetings once every few months.

How will a roundtable discussion take place from home without the 'backup' of the hallway talks?

Roundtable discussions via Zoom, and the like, will most probably be 'colder', yet we are still able to see one another, talk about issues, listen to one another and explain things. Employees still have a platform to express themselves. In other words, the basic advantages in these kinds of processes still exist and may take on an even greater meaning because they have a life of their own.

There are new topics opening up for discussion nowadays – What will the recruiting world look like in the new era? Which professions should work from home? What demands can we make of employees regarding their feelings of connection to the organization? What will make them feel connected to the company? Will employees' working hours become secondary, and they will be measured by their productivity and performance? How will employees be evaluated? Which tools should be used for evaluation, as we are connecting through a screen, unable to sense and see employees on a daily basis? How can we evaluate their social positioning in a group?

These are just some of the complex challenges regarding work-related relationships post-corona – the main issue being handling organizational distancing. In large companies, HR claim that part of the challenges will be solved by technology, which will make virtual meetings more accessible. For example, entering a room wearing 3-D glasses, which will enable you to see everyone and sit in a place of your choosing, creates a kind of closeness to reality – as we know it today.

There may also be a solution of coming to the workplace once a week or two for a mutual meeting, which would reduce the distance between the employee and the organizations.

Company owners, who for years vetoed the 'working from home' dilemma, have accepted the idea; for many of them working from home has aided their financial and business benefits. Employees, as well, have internalized the benefits of this new situation.

For some employees, working from home during the Coronavirus period has been life changing. Take for example, not having to travel to work every day. This allows for flexibility and convenience with regards to their working hours, leaving more time for other activities, like families, for example. Who would have thought that you could still work and have time to pick your children up from school and eat lunch with them?

In other words, any issue related to the employees' second circle of needs (which until now we have focused on from a completely different angle) will naturally be reinforced. Moreover, employees have the preference of choosing a place of employment. It is likely that a large number of employees will prefer working in places that allow, in one form or another, to work from home (freelance for example).

A large group of these part-time employees will help make professions with a high turnover rate, like call center representatives, much more flexible. Part-time jobs, which today are a lot less feasible, will allow more people to work – like mothers, students, the elderly, or anyone else who does not want to or cannot work eight hours a day.

If there would be jobs of four-hour shifts, then it would be possible for employees to combine different jobs. They would not need to focus on one thing but could study or even work at a different job at the same time, according to the hours that would suit them.

From a geographical distribution aspect, the above change would bring on great relief with regards to employee recruitment. For example, nowadays it is difficult to recruit employees from certain remote areas. These problems could be solved because of the changes brought on by Coronavirus. Physical proximity to the workplace would no longer be an issue.

The abolition of the importance of the geographical location will of course also extend to the rest of the world, opening cross-border employment opportunities. I cannot help but think about all Israelis, mainly young ones, living overseas and who are most probably not living the financial dream they had been hoping for, enabling them to make millions. This change will help them create more opportunities of income.

We Have Been Emoji Talking for a While Now!

In this future scenario, there will also be large differences in the scope of working from home between employees working at headquarters, technological employees, salespeople, call center and employee retention representatives. The scope will differ from one job to the other, and therefore our wisdom as employers, is to map out and create the optimal conditions for each job.

Working from home will also create new difficulties for some employees. Starting with blurring the line between home and work, as your living room may no longer be private territory, which may make things difficult, as well as culminating with a lack of the social needs usually fulfilled by the workplace. Some people go to their job to not only work, but also treat it as a social network for creating personal relationships.

Certain research shows that it is easier for young people to adapt to virtual communication; therefore, they find working from home quite natural.

If I take my peers and myself, for example – in other words the older adults – who are used to going into their colleague's office to ask after their family or to chat about work – these changes and upheavals affected us as well. Nowadays, we also finalize matters over the phone, send many text messages about personal and professional matters and use emojis.

Therefore, if you look in-depth, you will find that our personal interactions are becoming increasingly poor. This revolution is happening. We were heading that way regardless of Coronavirus, so there is no point trying to fight it.

The way I see the process is that we will still need, at least in the preliminary stages, to create some kind of unmediated contact, with certain frequency, between employees and their employers. In addition, there will be no escape in overcoming the many shortcomings to maintain the corporate culture and somehow bridge the distance. Until today, you could enter anyone's office, get a feel of the atmosphere, the energy and 'read' the person's body language. You could sense the nuances. To reach the same delicate understandings, we will need to encourage employees to talk more, directing the discourse to more participatory and precise places.

Another point that is relevant to the 'working from home' era, and HR is the response of management and company owners to these changes. As we know, in the first stage, companies dramatically cut down on their expenses: real estate, travel, dining rooms, AC, cleaning etc. Precisely from this place of money saving euphoria and expenditure cuts, companies might assume that they can reduce activities in HR and that working from home allows for employee welfare and retention to be redundant. My thoughts regarding these fears, which arise in many organizations, is that it will not happen here. We all talk about how difficult it is to see the effect corporate culture has on financial results. Under normal circumstances, this is a process that takes time until the outcome is evident, and in any case, you do not always connect the two – simply because, in many cases, it is uncomfortable to admit.

In my opinion, in this new situation the correlation between employee cultivation and financial tables will become evident in a much clearer, stronger, and quicker way. I believe that it will be evident in the company's results.

It is worthwhile thinking about it in the following way – even when employees go into their workplace on a daily basis, do not feel treated, nurtured or listened to, they are still inside a system, in a certain kind of inertia, giving the sense of belonging. Therefore, the harm caused to the company will be slow, subtle and harder to notice. Henceforth, if employees working from home do not feel a strong connection to their workplace and receive no extra treatment, they will be unmotivated to give it their best, or even to stay.

The bottom line is this, even if the conditions change, we remain the same people, with the same needs. As HR, we will need to meet employees' needs in greater intensity, in new ways and using different technologies.

Now, in the midst of the pandemic, we have established a professional steering committee, which, in a short time, is supposed to bring management recommendations for working from home in the future. Each team member of the committee was given a task to review a particular area, to conduct focus groups with employees, managers, and colleagues. So, despite this vague time, we are already examining what is next, to answer the following questions: Which roles should work from home? To what extent? What is the correct thing to do?

We plan to take the recommendations and conduct a pilot run in the field. What do you think will happen?

THE EFFECT OF CORONAVIRUS
ON OUR ORGANIZATIONS

Our workdays start almost as always. We begin our morning discussions with the same briefings, questions, challenges, and dilemmas. However, they are conducted via Zoom and there is an additional angle –addressing the difficulties arising due to working from home

Even roundtable discussions are conducted during this time, sometimes even more often than before, via Zoom of course. Using this platform as well, I prefer conducting the meetings in small groups of between 10 to 15 participants, to allow everyone the chance to express their opinion. As you know, when there is a large group, it is harder for people to open up, especially when it is done over virtual media. Anyone involved in these discussions is always briefed beforehand to sit with their team and department and discuss the topics they want to bring up in the discussion. Therefore, all participants come prepared to the discussions. The first topic in all discussions relates to the new working conditions – What is hindering the process? What is lacking? What is working? How can we improve the situation?

After conducting our current meetings with all levels of employees and after conducting a quick survey, we discovered that there are a few issues bothering employees. The main one, being extremely complex to my understanding, is the employee's lack of connection to the organization. It is definitely the most pressing problem, which needs to be addressed in all solemnity. This is about internal communications on all sides: from the ability to convey messages, information, and knowledge, to understanding the general aspects of what is going on and where things are headed.

As we said, when you are physically in the office, even if a rumor is spread around by the coffee machine, 'someone said something to someone', you can go to your manager's office, ask and get a direct answer. When you are working from home, matters can get complicated. Any question you do not get an immediate answer to, causes certain theories to develop in one's mind, which if shared with a coworker, may soon be shared with another coworker and in no time, a mountain is made out of a molehill. Therefore, through our discussions, we try our best to update employees, beyond the trivial information, about the financial statements and to share any new or unfamiliar data. We talk about how the company is handling the situation, how it is getting organized and what we foresee in the future.

Since we are all living in a vague world right now, even management, we do not know exactly what will happen, so we try our best to conduct tight communications with employees. Even if there is not a lot to update, it provides a sense of connection.

Trivia Competitions and Cheesecakes
In the meantime, the internal survey we conducted has shown gratifying facts on our side. The survey checked

how employees and managers perceived the speed and quality of the organization's handling of the new situation. The results were not surprising. We did get ahead of the market, getting organized three weeks before the 'Big Bang'. Among other things, we conducted a login connection test from all employees' homes to make sure there was not too heavy a load on the network and that it would all work. We defined assignments and teams, compiled name lists – definitely a thorough process. Therefore, when the alarm was raised, we were already prepared.

In fact, what complicated our activity and delayed us, with the rest of the country, were the vague guidelines from the government, some of which, as you are aware, were even contradictory. Therefore, we also took responsibility for areas in which instructions were supposed to come from outside and made decisions internally for them. For us, the key that guided and still guides us is maintaining our employees' health, and only then maintaining business continuity.

We continued working using the same format in the intermediate stages – between lockdowns and limitations. In the beginning, we thought of bringing more employees back to the office but we realized that we risked large-scale infections, which would obviously not only harm the employees' health, but ultimately if a whole department would be sent home, the business activity would be harmed as well.

Therefore, we created virtual communication activities with the employees inside their divisions and departments. For example, we showed videos of managers sharing their experiences and talking about how they are getting through these times, and how it is affecting them as managers. Through these videos, dilemmas are addressed. Employees, as well, have shared their own videos and presentations showing the difficulties and advantages of working from home. This was all done in order to strengthen the connection between the employees and the company.

HR personnel and managers are instructed by us to constantly connect with their employees who are working from home – to locate problems that may not be directly work-related. In the absence of direct contact, even a phone call showing some interest can pick up on someone's frame of mind. These situations, for example, need to be defined in a structured and organized format, preventing any bigger problems from arising.

We also carefully plan the days we meet at the office, which is an essential tool for communicating with the employees. These days must be dedicated to feedback, cross-sectional discussions, personal meetings, and briefings. Daily marathons will take place in different frequencies and should be structured in an organized and precise manner. Each day is planned according to the group that will be attending and it will be divided into sections.

In any case, the main goal for these frontal meetings is to interact – to see one another, to listen to each other and to hear out the employees.

In days like these, this is the way to create maximum connection to the company's agenda, activity, culture, and organizational vibe.

We are also all beginning to think of ways to conduct additional virtual meetings intended for fun and team building exercises, which also creates a connection between employees and the organization. For example, we have already held trivia games, a baking competition, which was broadcast live, workouts for the employees and in the near future, we plan to hold further leisure workshops.

In addition, we have added little touches of fringe benefits, like pizza, ice cream and flower deliveries for the employees and their families. These are not bombastic gestures – just displays of attention, simply to warm their hearts and our relationships.

Everyone enjoys the attention, but it is nothing to boast about in times like these. Here I come to an important point: Everyone understands that, at present, we are in an emergency situation. Many employees are grateful that effort is being made to maintain their employment, allowing them to work from home. At the time of writing this book, there are a million unemployed people in Israel. In our organization, we did not let a single employee go. Therefore, the current situation is somewhat different to whatever we have ever experienced before.

What happens when we get into a routine?

When the situation gets under control and we announce that the Coronavirus period is over, but we are continuing to work from home, it will take on a different angle. We are all human beings, and we all take indulgences for granted. Therefore, we will then have to deal with situations that are more complex.

We Will Have to Step Up Our Game!

We are constantly trying to figure out what is going on in the world, as we are all now in the same boat, searching for good ideas. Despite the fact that thousands of articles, opinions and surveys have been written about organizational distancing – it turns out that we are all still feeling our way in the dark, trying to understand the implications of it all.

Throughout the whole the Coronavirus period, I researched all the information I could possibly find from HR experts from large organizations as well as smaller companies. As I mentioned, nothing formal and structured has been written, but everyone is working on developing tools, including consulting firms and organizations that specialize in outdoor training as well as those that work in tandem with organizations in other ways.

The overall melody is that no one really knows what the future will bring, and each organization is simply managing the crisis from its own angle. Therefore, the only steadfast conclusion that can be drawn from the situation, in my opinion, is that from now on we will have to step-up our game regarding the organizational culture and strengthening employees' connections and relationships to their workplace.

This brings us to another substantial point – the organization of workers and social networks. In the presentation we introduced management to organizational distancing, we addressed the above aspect as well, and we showed that in terms of employee-management's relationships, there are two ways of looking at it. Let me just mention that the balance in the *seesaw model*, which we will continue to elaborate on in the following chapters, is also intended to prevent employees' dissatisfaction, sanctions and strikes. In the current situation, trying to locate the underground currents, which might cause the next outburst, is a much more complicated matter.

For the sake of illustration, let us say that there is a rumor going around that something is wrong with the company. When you are physically in the office, after approximately 15 people have heard the rumor, it will reach management's ears. At this point, the rumor is in its infancy, and we can respond, explain, douse the flames and most importantly diffuse the situation. With employees working from home, the rumor might begin to accumulate, eventually turning into a big mess. Not to mention the internal discourse that employees initiate, to which we are not exposed. If we also take into account that social networks today work hard and fast, and different factors from all sides have a lot more interests, rumors can flare up into serious outbursts before we can locate them.

On the other hand, committees and employee organizations will be at a greater disadvantage. Satisfied employees will show less interest and be less inclined to be dragged into situations that they were not bothered about in the first place. When you are sitting at home, far from the social pressures, situations are easier to manage, and you are less inclined to follow the herd. Therefore, the same situations that make it harder for management to communicate will also make it difficult for employee organizations.

More complex and in-depth procedures will also need

to be addressed differently. Issues that will be discussed at a later in this book, like introductory meetings with employees or identifying potential future managers, will be handled differently. In my opinion, precisely in the above areas we will need to use more measurable and structured tools, controlled procedures and ways to help us understand where to set the goal posts and which employees should be marked for development, retention and enrichment. In my opinion, it will become more of a technical and 'cold' process, losing the effect of 'gut feelings'. We will work more with our heads and less with our hearts.

Since we have mentioned here along the way that 'You should put your heart in management as well' – the challenge and paradox are revealed from this angle in full force as well. Once again, we revert to the big question: With all being said and done – how **do** you increase communication with your employees and create close, personal connections?

The answers to the above questions are still being written...

CHAPTER 2

**Assessment and Mapping
Inspired by
the *Seesaw Model***

"There are no shortcuts to any places worth going"
Beverly Sills

In order to illustrate the endless fluctuation in the working relationships between employees and management, we have chosen the image of a seesaw – in which the balance is always temporary

The model described here has six stages. These stages will be detailed in the following chapters.

When we talk about good and normal working relationships in an organization, regardless of whether there is a workers' committee, be it small or large – because these committees exist everywhere – we need to take constant care of our human resources to keep the system balanced. Hence the simple and basic conception of the *seesaw model*, claiming, as can be understood from the chosen image, that working relationships are dynamic, complex, affected by everything and charged with emotions.

To be honest, when it comes to working relationships and organizational culture, the warning lights go off many times when there is a crisis. After the fire has been lit, there are attempts to extinguish it using different resources, which are sometimes successful and other times not. However, often the fire that is extinguished is not necessarily the problem. Sometimes what erupts is very different from the main issue. Therefore, work–related relationships should not be handled on the spot, in a one-off manner, in the face of an incident or an event. These relationships need to be maintained on a regular basis – just like a seesaw.

We all know that working relationships are affected by the organizational culture and conduct, by the organization's atmosphere and agenda and the employees' general feelings towards these all. These make up one side of the seesaw. If this is the one side, naturally the other side should be the development and cultivation of human resources. After all, if I need to maintain a balanced working relationship, surely the weight needed to balance this all, would be the handling of human resources.

Do Not Just Check It Off Your List! Everything related to the general atmosphere of management, the behavior of the managers and their attitude towards the employees, which includes their development and cultivation, belong in this niche. Any one of these elements could affect the vibe in the organization and have a direct impact on the working relationships. If we could use a barometer to measure all this, we would see that any organizational move done in a good, correct, and genuine way – not just checked off a list – immediately balances out the dynamics.

If we look closely at what makes up working relationships, we will find that they include everything and affect everything. Every employee-manager interaction is a working relationship. This is the reality. Therefore, to balance and create the right situation, both in broad general terms as well as specific cases, we need to approach the matter through managerial and developmental tools.

There is Just a Little Something... Let us take, for example, a case where a problem arises between an employee and a manager. The optimal remedy would include taking care of the employee and, at the same time, providing the manager with the tools to solve the situation. In other words, we are balancing out the interaction between them.

The more we deal with the fluctuations in the temperament of the organization, understanding them and not being ashamed to admit problems exist, the more balanced the situation will be. Sometimes it is convenient to simply say, 'There is just a little something...' when below the surface there are raging fires burning.

This part of the developmental process and ongoing routine should exist in every organization. After all, we are talking about human beings and, in order to take care of them, management, who are running the business, and employees should have the tools and the space to do so in a proper manner.

Obviously, during the lifespan of every organization, there are ups and downs and everyone goes through crises and changes. From my experience, even in situations like these, when you enter a crisis, if the system is balanced, it is much easier to weather the storm. You can know and feel where the sensitivities lie, and if you have done a good job with organizational development, you will know which tools to use as well.

Just Leave Us Alone! There is no central axis in the model and in fact, there is no axis at all. Of course, it is management, and not employees, who have an influence and make decisions, but management can also lose control when the working relationships are out of sync. Examples of this are evident in Israel and around the world, mainly in view of the new employee organizations springing up.

Why are there eruptions?

Well, it is not because employees are happy and satisfied. It is obvious it results from distress. In my opinion, this is a cry saying, 'Look at us! Take notice of us, as we are part of the business. You cannot ignore us and not talk to us. You need to relate to us and take us into account.' Then usually when an employees' committee springs up, management become angry and are completely shocked, with the following narrative: 'How dare they? They should be grateful that they even have a salary.' After that, it can deteriorate to, 'What the hell? They cannot tell us who to fire and who not to, or what food to serve in the dining room. Who do they think they are?'

This is how it begins and, once the employees' committee gains strength and sanctions begin, management moves into panic mode, with the following, 'Okay. Let us give them what they want so that they leave us alone and let us be.' Obviously choosing this path is a mistake and will not solve the problem. It may calm the flames down at that specific moment – and on the surface, the seesaw may seem balanced, but in the long run, that is far from the case.

No Stopping on the Sides of the Road! This is actually a misconception that causes management to act in the following way: 'If the employees are unhappy, let's reach an agreement with them. Let's pay them some more money, add in a few perks and make them happy.' This is not the point though. What is needed is to change the atmosphere in the company, its culture and attitude. What is surprising, and in contrast to common opinion, is that it is not always about money. Money is a temporary solution, and the employer ends up paying more and more, while the working relationships remain unbalanced.

If you fail to understand that the real needs that exist, over and above money, begin and end with how management treats their employees, and everything is derived from that – you are lost!

The image of the seesaw was created to emphasize that there is constant movement. However, in actual fact, when I examine the system, it reminds me of some sort of a scale, with one difference though – the balance here does not stop – with what is called Perpetuum Mobile – perpetual mobility. Working relationships are a live mechanism; they are constantly changing with new factors impacting the equation all the time. Even a small, seemingly marginal event can turn into a tsunami, clouding the atmosphere and affecting the vibe like dominoes.

Therefore, as HR manager, you need to keep it all in constant balance. It is true that there will sometimes be events that will cause certain areas to heat up, as well as ups and downs. However, as long as you see and are aware of these events and feel in control knowing that you have supportive tools to help the balance, you will quickly be able to make an impact.

What is important to remember though is that the seesaw is constantly swaying! All the time. It does not take a break!

The Seesaw Model – Six Stages

STAGE 1 – Mapping the Strengths and Weaknesses in the Organization:
This is a crucial step in the process since its findings and results define all courses of action. This mapping process requires broad organizational vision, together with an ability to gather data, purifying it from interests and manipulations. An in-depth examination of each function in the company should be performed, to pinpoint all the personal and organizational weaknesses.

STAGE 2 – In Depth Assessment:
After we have mapped out and assessed the processes, products, technology and especially the organizational culture, we can move on to the in-depth assessment stage – using professional elements.

STAGE 3 – Analysis of the Findings:
Here we draw the current picture of the organization, which reflects its strengths and weaknesses and examine them against the vision and organizational strategy. This information allows us to assess and enhance the existing strengths. This is a different approach than those addressing the weaknesses alone.

STAGE 4 – Outdoor Activity to Complete the Picture and Construct a Development Plan:

To complete the mapping and assessment process, the findings should be analyzed and incorporated into operational actions. Outdoor activities can provide an accurate reflection of the employees, the skills, the competencies and the problems that characterize the units/teams in the organization. The findings of the outdoor activities will help build working plans for HR development.

STAGE 5 – Processes Following Assessment and Work Plans:

At this point, we return to the image of the seesaw – placing the employees and management or the committee and management on either side. Here a huge weight is placed on the work plans at the core of HR, because they have the power to produce positive dynamics.

STAGE 6 – Fruit Bearing Investment:

At this stage, the results of the relentless work in creating balance will be reflected. The good atmosphere and the built-up trust will ensure that crises can be overcome. Crises, as mentioned, will occur, since there is constant motion, yet they will not happen suddenly and unexpectedly.

When describing the working relationships as a kind of seesaw, we are in fact describing the power struggle that has erupted between the parties – powers that are seemingly opposite – maybe even hostile. The supremacy of the one (management) is the inferiority of the other (employees/committee), but this is not the case in actual fact. On our seesaw, there is constant motion, never-ending. An action taken for the welfare of the employees gathers momentum, ensuring the employees' willingness to meet management halfway in the next movement. For example, in cooperation with the signing of new wage agreements, enhancing every employee's personal motivation and strengthening their sense of belonging and loyalty to the company, places the employee in the center of the action.

As mentioned, in the following chapters we will elaborate on the different aspects of the model – beginning with the first stage.

CHAPTER 3

Mapping the Strengths and Weaknesses

It is Not All Theory!

(THE THREE INITIAL STAGES OF THE MODEL)

"A prudent question is one-half of wisdom"

Francis Bacon

In the mapping and assessment process, there are, of course, ground rules that cannot be broken. However, the 'best assessment tool' is the one that we feel is effective, proven by experience and works best in the specific situation and time. Here are some suggestions which, from my experience, are effective

A few years ago, whilst in a board meeting, I was asked to describe the assessment and mapping process I was about to undertake in the company. At the end, during the Q&A, one of the participants exclaimed, "Wow! It sounds like a detective thriller movie." Up to that point, that image did not entered my mind. "I mean, there are facts to be found in all the layers," the creative VP continued, "and some are hidden and need to be exposed, confirmed and crosschecked."

"Actually, it reminds me of a psychologist peeling away layers," someone else commented, while another participant claimed that for some reason it reminded him of a crossword puzzle. Another manager compared the process to a medical diagnosis. They were all correct! The assessment and mapping process is part of the data collection stage, which includes all the characteristics mentioned above.

There are many models for the assessment process and during the years, I have found myself gathering and collecting information from here and there, examining situations. Some of the methods are based on theories and other models, while others are based on my gut feeling. With time, you learn what works better, enabling you to build your own assessment and mapping model, which is sometimes hard to confine into a defined frame, and not necessarily the only one to be used for guidance.

Therefore, I am not suggesting one single method here. If you have a method that you believe in over and above the one mentioned here or feel more comfortable with at a certain point – great! I believe that it is worthwhile to invest in examining different models and checking different tools, eventually using the accumulated experiences, which, in my eyes, are the best teachers – to see what really works at the end of the day.

What experience has clearly taught me, and what is true also in the area of assessment and mapping, is that in every process you need to act with 'both feet on the ground'. In other words, on the one hand you can abstractly examine theories but, on the other hand, it is important to maintain a steady foothold on the ground to be able to go back and examine situations at eye level and see how they can be applied in reality. If we decide only to act according to the models, as good and clear as they may be, we risk the chance of running into the sad fact that the world is not always built accordingly. There are basic, rooted, and fundamental situations with milestones impossible to escape during a process.

It is my belief that no one particular tool is 'the best assessment tool', so therefore I will not provide a single defined model. However, I will give examples of components that are important to have within the process – to get the most out of any tool.

The methods that I mention here regarding the assessment and mapping process include – personal conversations; roundtable discussions; attending team meetings; 'freestyle field trips'; outdoor events; obtaining advice from external consultants; the 4X4 Model; using feedback and enrichment programs from previous years; using the strengths and weakness model; comparing parallel companies from the same industry; gathering relevant information from academic institutions; gathering stories from accumulated field experience.

> *"Most people do not listen with the intent to understand; they listen with the intent to reply"*
>
> **Stephen Covey**

Be Smart and Be Quiet!
It will be Worth Your While!

Not everyone can both assess and map out, as well as draw conclusions to build plans. There is no need to multitask. If there is a certain field that you are less proficient in, or feel less comfortable with, consult with professionals who are experts in these fields. Indeed, in my opinion, it is convenient that everything eventually merges into one expert who synchronizes everything – which of course does not negate receiving help in other areas.

My professional biography states otherwise. Since I had to do everything on my own, I learned by going through the motions. Luckily for me, most of the time it was successful, but it is definitely not the only way. In several cases, I took a chance – sometimes it was calculated, and at other times, I was unaware I was taking a risk. Sometimes it also takes luck!

My first suggestion when doing an assessment relates to a general tendency – talkativeness. When going through the process of assessment, it is best to do as little talking as possible; to open your ears and eyes more than your mouth. Even if you are used to beginning a discussion with your own decisive statements – look and listen. From true listening, you will not only hear what is said and what is not being said, but you will mainly catch on to the 'how' – how things are expressed, the general vibe and what can be read between the lines. I internalized this insight during one of the most insightful and empowering workshops which I participated in.

My professional path was cultivated through the participation in courses in Israel as well as around the world. I went all the way to Singapore for an Executive Excellence Workshop and that was when I learned the rationale behind the importance of listening. Their explanation states that if you have been chosen to be a manager, then you are valued and highly thought of. Therefore, you can afford to talk less in the beginning. This is a tip that in time turned out to be golden!

So, teach yourself first and foremost to listen. It will make you less intimidating, and easier to read and cooperate with, creating a better atmosphere. By the way, even on a personal level, silence should not be taken for stupidity. Someone whom I admire a lot taught me that it is better for you to be asked to speak, than told to be silent. How true is that!

From the beginning of the process, it is worth examining and paying attention to all levels of the organization, and not just focusing on management, thus falsely leading you to believe that you are aware of what is happening throughout the company. This will only reflect, at best, what is happening in management. Go down to the lower levels – to the level of the divisions and departments and introduce yourself – that is all you need. Go as a spectator to listen and learn.

Puzzles and Crosschecking Information, Which Direction is the Wind Blowing?

Today, in retrospect, after working for many companies, I understand that I have always worked using the 'puzzle' method and for me, it is the most precise method.

In the first company where I worked as an HR manager, I developed in the organization, eventually landing this position, so I was unaware as to whether my method actually worked or if things were happening because I knew the system. I was not sure whether the model and its method would have worked in any company, without having any prior knowledge. This was definitely my biggest fear when I began my next job as VP of HR in a large company.

To my delight, within a short time period, I managed to conduct a mapping process and, in a presentation, showed findings that were less pleasant about the company. Once the presentation was done, there was a tense silence. However, after a short while, one of the more veteran VPs stood up and said, "I don't understand how, after such a short time, you succeeded in showing us an accurate picture, with all the nuances, and everything that is hiding below the surface. These are things which would have taken us years to reveal."

It was only then that I admitted to myself that the assessment method that extends across the whole organization, and includes many meetings, from the employee level to the VP level and basically collects from each a small piece of the puzzle – probably works. Of course, this includes the contexts and connections that come after putting all the parts together, because it is only after hearing one angle and then another, that you can build the correct picture.

The more experience you gain, the quicker you understand the meanings and weight of things said during the assessment process. The criteria are, for example, the intensity of what is said and how it is said. What is the role of the person talking? Do you plan on setting up other meetings with them?

Therefore, if I meet a manager who claims to have an issue with their employee's conduct, I try to understand how the other managers also view the situation and then I will move on to hear from the employees. Obviously if more than one employee is of the same opinion, then there is most likely a problem.

Next, I will try to understand how the problem came about and assess the best way to handle it. It is not always a matter of who is responsible for the problem, but how it manifests itself. Too big a gap between the managers' versions and those of the employees are typical in companies in which there is no open dialogue.

"Facts from paper are not the same as facts from people"

Harold Geneen

PERSONAL DISCUSSIONS NOT ALL AT ONCE!

The mapping process should begin with personal interviews with employees from all sectors, from all ranks, and from all levels. The personal interviews should be pleasant and informal

The conversations should include intentional questions, without being too direct, but ones from which it will become clear what you want to infer.

Examples for questions:

- What is the prevailing culture?
- Does the organization have a closed or open door policy?
- Are meetings being conducted with managers?
- Do managers liaise with employees?
- Is there the option to challenge authority?
- Is there managerial courage?
- How much do the employees feel they can influence a situation?
- Do the employees feel they are able to do their job in the best way possible?

You need to ask many questions.

Usually, the employees will be apprehensive in the beginning of the meetings. The ice needs to be broken as quickly as possible and an informal, open and free atmosphere and context for the dialogue should be provided, thus increasing the chance to receive meaningful answers.

Stop with the Hypocrisy If discussions are conducted in an open manner, there is a high chance that the truth will come out, and not only the things they want you to hear. This is a point that needs to be seriously considered. I have had more than enough discussions, especially with the upper ranks, which were conducted in a politically correct, fake, and stiff manner. I had to intervene by saying – "come on, let's talk about how things really are." Of course, you can purposely activate the change of direction once you have met with the levels below, together with the rest of the organization. Then you will have enough tools to make it clear to the other side 'we know what we are taking about.'

A Discussion – Not an Interrogation! Usually, it is worthwhile to soften up anyone who presents an unrealistic, too good to be true picture with a sentence like – 'I have heard other points of view as well', all the while making sure not to turn the discussion into an interrogation. It must be made very clear that this is just an assessment to be used only to find out what needs to be taken care of in the company.

As assessors, we need to remember that the more the sensitive issues are handled, even when they are less pleasant – as you know, people tend not to want to deal with the less pleasant sides of things – the more accurate the assessment will be. On the other hand, when dealing with flaws and failures, do not neglect the strengths of the organization – to balance the energy you invest in downsides. The positive aspects must be maintained because nothing should be taken for granted. There are organizations in which you see incredible achievements, but they are not in the spotlight enough, which is also a serious mistake.

Have a Laugh at Your Expense! In the beginning of the personal discussions you should start by scattering the clouds of 'What the hell is going on here?!' Most people arrive at these discussions very cautiously, especially if this is the first time, they have been summoned to such a procedure. So, you need to create the right, pleasant atmosphere, by laughing about yourself, relating a few personal stories about yourself, and basically doing whatever it takes to establish a rapport with everyone. Once you have loosened up a bit and the conversation starts to open up, you will naturally feel more relaxed and many times the employees may say something they had not meant to disclose to you.

It is at this point that many interviewers make the mistake of pouncing on the issue immediately – to interrogate and learn more. I recommend avoiding that, because usually when you point the conversation in that same direction, the employee in front of you will close up. It will be clear that you are onto something that should not have been mentioned in the first place.

Approach the issue in a different way, from a different angle. You need to know how to manage the information flowing your way. You need to be considerate, not to rush but to take your time. It is better if you miss something you thought was important, rather than messing up the whole meeting. Remember that you could come across the employees in the hallway or in team meetings. There are other situations in which you will have the opportunity to figure out any matters. If it is something real and crucial, it will pop up in another form and in another place. Taking the high road and not reacting immediately, just making a mental note of the issue, is the best road for all.

Breaking the Ice, A Smile and a Gut Response!

When you are conducting a personal discussion, it is important to remember that you need to lead the conversation. At the same time, you need to make it as informal as possible, whilst directing the discussions to places that are not only comfortable, but also provide information – mainly of the discreet kind. The questions should be cautious but intentional, as you do not always know in which direction this will take you. One question, for example, can deal with the frequency in which employees meet with their direct and senior managers. There have been cases where the response to such a question was a bitter laugh and comments like – 'Do I meet with my manager every day? Of course not!' 'When did I last see my manager's manager? Wow! A long time ago – maybe a few months ago.' 'With the VP? Maybe in the last quarter.' 'The CEO? I have been in the company for 15 years and I have no idea what he looks like.'

CEO with No Salary I have recognized throughout the years, and from the many discussions, that one of the more important decisions is that it is worthwhile to come prepared with a question that the employee will not be expecting. This way they are pushed into a corner, and you will gain a response that comes straight from their gut. My method of operation goes more or less like this – 'Okay, I am now appointing you to be CEO of the company, but without the

salary.' This already triggers a smile, breaking the ice some more. Then I continue – 'And you can decide whatever you want. One decision. What would you change in the company?'

Usually, in the beginning, they are taken aback, sometimes even becoming speechless. 'Hold on, change with regards to myself? Or...'

I direct them a little – 'No, no. In the company. You are CEO now.'

There are rare occasions in which they have difficulty reaching any decision to the above question, but there are many occasions when their responses have amazed me, and I have found myself wondering how they reached such accurate assessments. These responses sometimes come from employees who are nowhere near the relevant levels to have been able to recognize these issues with such clarity. They ask questions such as – 'Why do the managers not really address any issues? Why are we not allowed to speak our mind? Why are our opinions not considered?' Hearing such insight makes you realize that everything is already out in the open and there is no need to peel back the layers.

From this point, the issues that lead to the main problems in the organization begin to pop up.

THEY Started It! As a side note, it is worthwhile mentioning that, besides the information you receive at this point, something else is gained on the way. When employees see that a short while after bringing up a sore subject in the discussion the organizational culture begins to change and managers are suddenly applying 'open door' policy, or more co-working teams are being formed and are taking an interest in their stand, they will feel like they have had an impact – that their voices have been heard.

Of course, there are marginal cases where, in response to the question of being appointed CEO, the responses are – 'I would give all employees a pay raise.' Then I challenge them by asking – 'What happens if the company begins to collapse, eventually causing it to shut down, would you still give everyone a pay raise?' Usually, following this response, they back down from their joyful cries of a virtual raise and bring up other issues.

Only a small percentage of the employees respond by complaining and letting off steam in the form of 'THEY started it!' With these employees, I tend to raise a counterpoint, and indirectly, gently turn the spotlight on to the question of what the employees' part is in what goes on in the company – how responsible are they for what is happening? Of course, I do so while noting factually that the CEO, managers, and senior ranks have a crucial effect. Yet still, as employees, they should ponder on where they stand in this operation. As human beings, we have constant tendencies to know exactly what the other person should be doing.

In any case, as mentioned, it is usually a minor group of

employees complaining. The vast majority will enlighten you. From my experience, in certain companies you can even hear statements like – 'We do not take enough advantage of our professional capabilities in developing new products,' or 'We do not provide good enough service.' Statements like these, ought to be made by senior management, so when you hear them coming from the different levels in the organization – it is amazing!

> *"Do actions agree with words?*
> *There's your measure of reliability.*
> *Never confine yourself to the words"*
>
> **Frank Herbert**

More Credibility, Less Stuttering!

The issue of credibility is also expressed in the personal discussions; after all, in every personal interaction with employees you are not just the questioning party, but also the respondent. Let us take, for example, situations in which a company is rumored to be going through a streamlining process but nothing operational has really happened. You can, so to speak, beat around the bush with them by saying something like – 'No, it is nothing...There are only talks at this point...' simply because you know that it is going to be a long process and you do not want to enter an unpleasant conversation at that moment.

In my opinion, rather than stuttering, it is better to present things as they are and formulate a response like

– 'Yes, it may very well be that we are going to have to deal with a streamlining process, but I can guarantee you that it will be done in the most fair and humane way possible and not like a thief in the night.' In other words, reality must not be evaded even if it is blurry and painted in pink. This is not the correct thing to do – especially not in the long run!

Maybe Others are Better? Another common example is, during a discussion when an employee will complain, directly or indirectly, about their manager. The best way to handle it is to give an explanation in the following way – 'Look, this is not a discussion about your manager, but as a company we will not keep on managers who are found to be unsuitable to the culture we are trying to create here.' In other words, you are letting them know that you have heard the complaint, but you will not allow employees to dish on one another. However, as a concept, you are conveying another message that is important to understand and that is the organization is not scared to deal also with executive levels. The trend is the same and the requirements are valid for the entire organization – maybe even more so for managers.

Another example of the breach of trust is by evading unpleasant answers, which can occur when an employee sits down and says – 'It cannot be that I did not receive such and such when everyone else did...' The answer, in my opinion, should begin with repeated questions – 'Maybe you have yet to prove that you are good enough? Maybe you have not been trying hard enough? Maybe the others are better?' Then you should add – 'Do you agree with me that it is only fair and reasonable that there is differentiation in the system? After all, if everyone receives the same, the organization will be mediocre.'

This is not an easy situation to be in, because this employee did not receive the same as his or her peers and is taking it on a personal level. Therefore, your response should not be blunt or offensive, and definitely not belittling, just the opposite – do your best to empower them. In other words, the message conveyed should be – 'From the place you are at now, you have room to grow. Do not look at others but look at yourself and your performance. Think about what you could do differently to be compensated according to how much you think you deserve.'

When you offer an unobtrusive, embracing and enabling approach, albeit a determined one, you have a good chance to convey a credible statement with the hope and possibility for growth.

Concentration and Dispersion, What is the Daily Prescription?

I recommend spreading out the personal discussions throughout the day and not conducting them in sequence, otherwise it will feel like a factory line. Employees should not see a line outside your door, allowing them to ask themselves and others questions like 'What? Are we in line at the HMO?' It looks too artificial and misses the mark.

I think you also need time to become focused in the discussion, especially when you are talking with an employee summoned to meet with you out of the blue, and so it takes time to dispel the cloud of suspicion. What is more, the assessor is also required to show a lot of sensitivity and attentiveness to soften the atmosphere and, after not too many questions, should know how to separate the grain from the chaff.

I spread the discussions out, not meeting with more than four employees a day. Marathon meetings will also affect the right way you filter and distill the information – a process to which you need to dedicate time. The information needs to sink in and be processed properly.

During the mapping process, you should also conduct roundtable discussions, team meetings, management meetings and field trips, which allows everything to be connected. This enables you to sharpen your perspective from discussion to discussion.

"The most important thing in communication is to hear what isn't being said"

Peter Drucker

ROUNDTABLE DISCUSSIONS
TAKE NOTE!

At a later stage, after you have conducted several personal discussions and have more of an idea of how the organization is built, it is worthwhile to begin conducting roundtable discussions, which should include employees from different levels, to encourage open dialogue. Roundtable discussions are a powerful tool that can be used for different needs. From my experience, it is effective also for the mapping process

Obviously, there are substantial differences between one-on-one meetings and the dynamics in these discussions. When it is one-on-one, employees are usually more relaxed; when it is with a group of people, a different vibe takes place, in which the atmosphere can change constantly.

These roundtable discussions definitely provide an opportunity for the employees to be heard, even if most of the time, at least in the beginning, it is only venting and complaining, which you will need to know how to direct and neutralize. This can be done by preparing the exact topics for discussion and by managing the discussion in a sensitive yet determined manner. By the way, a healthy degree of bickering could be cathartic; just make sure to keep the situation under control.

From one of the trainings I took part in, I adopted the

recommended method of writing down where everyone was sitting. Over the years, I have found this not only to be efficient but also to shorten the processes. Therefore, anyone watching from the side will see me writing, sketching, marking the places around the table. I write down the names and roles of those present, and then add notes about each one, mostly relating to their body language and tone of voice – how each one reacts when another is talking; are they attentive or do they hear without relating? All of these contribute to the puzzle.

Today these markings can also be refined and photographed, with pictures added to the lists, which helps you connect to the situation much quicker. In any case, even if it is only a name and description to help remind you of the person – take notes. I have also developed markings of my own. For example, if there is someone relatively noticeable who catches everyone's attention, I take note of that, as well as the opposite – if there is someone who nobody seems to listen to, I mark that down as well. This method is effective in all aspects – for collecting personal information, organizational dynamics, and other issues, some visible and others not so much.

Now Let's Count Knowledge and Experience

When summoning a group for a roundtable discussion, you encounter the same phenomenon as with the personal discussions. The participants withdraw into themselves, wondering what they are really doing there, and even though they have been asked to come prepared with questions and topics they would like to raise, they come ready for battle.

The way they analyze the situation is that they see senior management personnel and assume they are going to be tested in some way. There are ways in which this redundant tension can be defused. I, for one, already in the beginning of the discussion, ask all those present to introduce themselves.

My questions are direct – 'Tell us about your job and where you come from. How long have you been working in the company?' We sit and let each employee elaborate on their answers to the above. Then I spring a surprise they do not suspect at all and ask them – 'Tell me how many years of experience there are in this room? Where can I buy such experience? From what university can it be achieved? From what recruitment plan can I bring the intelligence that is here in this room?'

Then usually I add something along the lines of – 'Don't get confused! The brains are not only found on the top floors of the building. Besides undergoing managerial training, the people sitting up there are just like you, and today they hold positions that you may achieve as well. One thing is for sure, it does not make them any smarter.'

We all know that seniority can often be perceived as an obstacle, with thoughts like – 'I am a veteran and therefore no longer count; I am not taken into consideration as much and I am just taken for granted now.' In this case, I turn the tables and it works.

I take the issue that is perceived as a weakness and turn it into a strength about which they had not thought. After this dialogue, I always look around to see their faces, looking at one another and, from the relaxing of their mouths and their body language, it is evident that they are less tense, and definitely more relaxed. This is when they begin to realize that this time they are being approached from a different angle. They are being spoken to in a different language. All of a sudden, they are being told that their worth is no less than the managers', and that there is great value to what they contribute — their knowledge and experience, and moreover, they are being asked to talk about them.

This is a turning point in the discussion.

"Everyone you meet knows something you don't know but need to know. Learn from them"

Carl Jung

'Freestyle Field Trips'
Discussions from the Field

In addition to the roundtable discussions I initiate, I also conduct what is called 'freestyle field trips', in which I interact with the employees, in their physical workspace, while they do their actual work

The sessions are conducted in a completely unstructured, non-methodological way, in the form of an open discussion, with general questions – 'How are you doing? What are you doing?' 'Can you show me how it is actually done?'

With time and experience, your radar adjusts to their body language, behavior and the reference and manner in which they perceive their roles – however minor. The way the employees present things matters; what tools they have when dealing with problems and how they handle them. If you observe correctly, you can absorb a lot from this information. The more employees, roles, and places you meet in the organizational hierarchy – the better and more focused the feedback you will receive.

Another means I often use is to join in the different meetings – team meetings, departmental meetings as well as divisional and managerial meetings, even if they are morning meets with employees. I participate only as a spectator to observe the dynamics. When someone comments about something, are they heard or dismissed? Are guidelines presented in a clear manner?

Is there a message of 'we are all in this together' conveyed or one of 'go and manage on your own'? Are leadership qualities being exhibited?

The higher the ranks of the employees participating in the meetings, the more you must pay attention to the personas, the managers' managers, until you reach the level of VP. Although you are sitting in the meetings as a colleague, it is important, at least in the initial stage of the assessment, to keep your distance and to look at the bigger picture in order to see how things are being conducted.

This is the point where you begin to map how decisions are made – how much place is given to opinions that are not mainstream, how much patience and tolerance is revealed and do the employees stand up for themselves. Is it a matter of persona or policy? You can decipher all these facts with clarity if you position yourself as a bystander, without becoming involved.

"The problems are solved, not by giving new information, but by arranging what we have known since long"

Ludwig Wittgenstein

A Model that Makes Sense and Aims Straight for the Heart

Another tool I tend to use in the assessment and mapping process is derived from Bohlander & Snell's mapping model for human capital architecture. It is a tool that suited our needs and we made it a multi-evaluative tool. In my opinion, it is easy to apply, examining the real situation in depth and with accuracy and has huge advantages – it is less biased than executive evaluations, easy to understand, and very visual

Bohlander & Snell, experts in the field of HR management, developed the model to strategically identify the human resources in an organization. The model presents four distinguishable employee types: core knowledge workers; traditional job-based employees; alliance/partners; and contract labor. In each segment I embed the relevant information, to learn how to treat the different populations, knowing that a match needs to be made between the measuring tool and the specific type of population.

Obviously, the model does not stand on its own when dealing with the organization but is always part of the process. In fact, we use the model only after we have conducted most of the personal discussions and roundtable discussions and joined in the team meetings. At the same time, we gather additional information to be used in the model, which includes questionnaires we have handed out to managers.

The questionnaires ask managers, colleagues, and external collaborators to fill in a table that rates the characteristics of the company's roles from 0-6. They indicate, among other things, the importance of the roles, what learning curve is required for them and how long it takes; what level of professionalism and requirements are needed etc.

When you add up all these parameters, you actually get numbers that are easy to work with and you can start placing them on a map. Since the table is about ranking the necessity of the various roles, a mapping of the core roles is obtained.

Strengths VS Weaknesses, Stop the Volunteers!

One of the critical findings in the assessment and mapping process is discovering the strengths and weaknesses in the organization, and I include them in the model as well. They both need to be dealt with separately. The natural way of thinking is that when we find strong points and strengths, we should leave them be, turning our full attention to the weaker areas. This is a common mistake to be avoided, because precisely this cultivation of strengths – important as they are on their own – can be used as a springboard to solving problems.

A point of strength can consist of different kinds of elements. For example, if the employees feel connected and identify with the company and its brand. There are companies in which I have worked, where employees had such strong connections to the company's brand that they did not dare bring any other brand into their homes. It was embedded so strongly into the organizational culture, and at each company event, it was amazing to see how the employees' first concern at any organizational event was that the products were 'our products'.

This strong point is not only about the product itself, but the employees' emotional connection to the company and how they relate to it. In one company, we got tangible evidence to the strength of such a connection, after organizing what was called 'going into the field'. It was during one of the Jewish Holidays, which is always a high point in the sales of that company's products. We wanted to encourage sales in different stores, and therefore needed to recruit stewards, assistants and sales promoters.

We asked the employees if anyone wanted to volunteer, while ignoring the pessimists around us who claimed that no one would come forth if they were not going to be paid. To cut a long story short – in the end, we had to filter out and reduce the flow of volunteers, because the stores were asking us not to send any more stewards. The numberamount of volunteers was overwhelming. Even retirees wanted to volunteer, and employees begged to bring their family members with them. It was an amazing connection! The quality of such an organization needs to be brought to the forefront, strengthened, and used as an example.

Striving for Mediocrity, Caution!
Area Too Hot!

Once you have located the weaknesses in an organization, and every organization has their fair share of them, you need to invest in dealing with them. On every level, there are those employees who need to be retained. It is worthwhile checking, for example, if the senior engineer, who does excellent work, participates in enough training to keep up to date with the ever-advancing technology.

There are always burning issues as well. For example, in one company we found that a large part of the HQ divisions like finance, HR, administration and security, did not have a clear incentive plan or precise and measurable goals and management skills were at an extremely low level. This was to such an extent that we found some divisions headed by managers only by virtue of their position in the hierarchy, lacking basic management tools in their toolbox. They had no idea how to conduct discussions with their employees, or how to convey organized guidelines or manage a structured team meeting. It turned out that, because of this, bad management had been running the company for years. By the way, this is a common phenomenon in many organizations.

Other common weaknesses that I have encountered repeatedly are places that have turned into 'islands' and acted like bubbles inside the organization. Since they do not have any specific problems, in time they get to a stage of what I call – 'striving for mediocrity' – an area that is neither bad nor outstanding, so it is convenient not to be dealt with. These 'islands' have a will of their own in which they have developed their own style of management and conduct, remaining on the same level of achievements and results for years. These employees do not push themselves nor go out of their way to change anything.

This phenomenon is encountered mainly in large organizations, and you usually find that these 'islands' geographically are also remote, located in faraway corners, where outside visitors do not usually go. This is a separate world incorporated into the organization. It is bad for several reasons: you have less control over what is happening, and many things go unnoticed. In addition, these employees tend to be pulled into more comfortable zones rather than having to strive for something more. They do not necessarily get dragged down nor dodge responsibility, but the mediocrity becomes a warm and convenient place. This is exactly the stage in which you need to stand up and remind them – 'Beware, guys, this warmth is not really comfortable!'

This phenomenon needs to be handled by change and job swapping, with lots and lots of attention and most carefully, especially as we are all afraid of change, particularly in the unstable work world these days.

Preservation and Internal Departure, Was or Was Not?

Another difficult problem that can be detected relatively quickly, especially by the mapping model included in the assessment, is identifying employees who have cut off contact, and are present-absent. These are employees we refer to as 'departed internally' – a concept derived from the Israeli Kibbutz2 and describes people who have socially distanced themselves, but it relates to the working world as well. It is an employee leaving only an illusion of their presence – something like the cat's smile from Alice in Wonderland.

How do we find someone who is, but who actually is not?

Since the map is visual, many times at the mapping stage, this phenomenon stands out. From there, one has to check whether it is due to a monotonous job, or has to do with the employees themselves. To find this out, we continue examining the employees – checking their level of participation in activities, if they are involved in the workplace and so on and so forth. During personal discussions, which managers should hold frequently, employees with 'one foot out the door' can easily be detected.

I have found that the more companies grow and the more their employees mature through the years, the higher the chance of finding a large group of employees who have mentally checked out. When you take an in-depth look, you usually find employees with lots of capabilities and knowledge, yet most of them have

2. A kibbutz (lit. "gathering, clustering") is a collective community in Israel that was traditionally based on agriculture.

found themselves sinking into monotony throughout the years and sometimes they simply do not make any extra effort. It is a matter of character – not everyone is ambitious – as you know. Some people come to work, do what they need to do and nothing more.

To my understanding, this is harmful to everyone. Obviously, the organization loses manpower, often of a very high quality, and it is especially bad for employees with 'one foot out the door'. Coming every day, punching in and just doing what is necessary then punching out – can make one's day-to-day quite depressing.

Once it is clear who the potential leavers are, we focus on them and get them motivated. I have found that sometimes, left in their own world of content, but moved to a different seat, can instill some life. Sometimes, for the sake of mobility to enrich and refresh, it is worthwhile building enrichment paths and performing moves of job swapping between positions.

The optimal action is for potential leavers to be combined into working groups, which are mainly heterogeneous groups, with employees from different jobs and roles. Sometimes these groups can be formed at the roundtable discussions while at other times a different format is needed. In any case, there needs to be a platform for employees to express themselves and contribute to the discourse of their worlds, which usually strengthens the employees on individual levels in an incredible way.

We repeatedly see this phenomenon. These employees, who have hardly been seen or heard, suddenly flourish. They feel relevant. Obviously, there are some that no matter what you try to do – nothing helps, but from my own professional individual statistics, this genuinely has a positive impact on the majority. You can get so much more out of these employees!

The outcome of this process can also be heard from the managers. They are sometimes extremely surprised at what they have 'right at home' and, as a direct result, they begin to look at their employees in a different light. A whole circle is created – one that, as managers, we are required to incorporate in the organizational culture.

One Picture Blabbers a Thousand Words!

To validate the mapping process, I try as much as possible to approach companies from the same worlds of content and ask them to fill in the tables. This way, I know how the situation in my company compares to the professional field I want to analyze. This crosschecking provides another level of accuracy.

At the same time, I also turn to employment agencies to gather more information, because here there are elements of core roles and generic ones, and a clear picture of the level of recruitment is necessary. The core includes the leading and unique roles in a certain industry.

For example, professions like HR and finance are usually generic roles (even though it is not nice to shoot oneself in the foot), because employees in these fields can be replaced relatively easily. Of course, certain expertise is necessary, but this is less specific and not as unique as a high-voltage engineer, for example, required in some of the companies I have worked in. So, you want to see what the market situation is for the core roles in terms of recruitment ability and the scope and scale of their demands.

The element that completes the environmental puzzle is contacting university institutions. I provide a list of the required roles to the relevant academics, and they give me data, which clarifies where the professions with the highest demand are. This is an important parameter in the mapping level, and sometimes even in the operational level, like recruiting a large amount of students, which happened in one of the companies.

After gathering and crosschecking all the information we receive, we begin to map out the different circles.

Sometimes it turns out that the model requires many circles to support the full picture and focus it. The size of the circle, for example, indicates the number of employees inside it. In places with very large groups, it could be productive to divide them up into another resolution to see if the whole group does actually belong in the same circle, which in reality signifies how core their roles are.

Even at this high level of detail, you encounter positions that belong in the top right circle as well as in the circle on the left, or even at the bottom – two completely different places in terms of their core rank.

What is obtained from all these mappings on the model?

Plenty! From a strategic point of view, there is nothing more convenient and clearer than this model. You can see a picture in front of your eyes, a snapshot that immediately highlights the general situation. It has already been said and rightly so, that a picture is worth a thousand words. Suddenly, you can see the groups, their sizes and even details indicating which employees, and how many, are in need of retention and special attention.

How Can an Engineer Be Engineered?

I came across an excellent example of the power and importance of the mapping achieved through Bohlander & Snell's model while working in a very large company. After gathering all the data and spreading it out in the model, it became apparent that one of the key roles in the organization was that of an electrical engineer specializing in high voltage. In that company at that time, there were only four such engineers even though there was a need for many more. After examining the reason behind this lack of personnel, we found that engineering was a sought-after profession, extremely difficult to find professionals for, and almost no training was available for it.

In addition, we found that out of the four engineers in the company, three were supposed to retire within a year. This is an example of a crisis that, if not for the mapping, would not have been revealed, because the engineers had been working smoothly for years and so no one had considered the size and urgency of the problem. Initially we thought there was no issue and engineers could be recruited from other places. However, it very quickly turned out that the companies in the field, like the *Israeli Electrical Company* and other infrastructure companies, were all competing for the same limited population.

We realized that we had to prepare ourselves in a way we had never done before. We reached out to one of the universities with expertise in the field and located students who had two years left for them to get their degree. We funded their studies after signing them on as a commitment to come work for us.

In fact, we could have found ourselves facing a huge crisis without have seen it coming at all. The mapping shows the main, conspicuous issues. You can see the exact size of a group and can therefore build a better, more professional, and goal-oriented plan for their training, treatment, and support.

Given the fact that we are ultimately talking about a business organization, the exact specific needs must be identified and tailored to suit the right positions in the right places.

"Coming together is the beginning.
Keeping together is progress.
Working together is success"
Henry Ford

STYLES OF MANAGEMENT
HOW IS THE CHAIN CONNECTED?
(THE THIRD STAGE OF THE MODEL – ANALYSIS)

Split management and managers who are only interested in their immediate gain cause damage to an organization. A small tale about a crate illustrates such a lack of connection well

Here is a story that illustrates how the stages of the organizational analysis help locate problems in managers' conduct. In one of the organizations, we began the assessment stage with discussions that I held with the VPs, but they did not manage to help me understand what was actually happening in the company, although they claimed there were problems. During the process, which included personal discussions with the employees, roundtable discussions, sitting in on meetings and field trips, we tried to decipher the organizational culture.

We wanted to understand what the management style was, where the underground currents were and how the politics of the organization worked. Slowly, as the data was collected, I began to map problems at the level of the guidelines going down the chain – the way messages were being conveyed. Surprisingly, each time I did an in-depth examination of a group belonging to a certain level, I realized that the problem stemmed from the level above. Therefore, I went up and up, until I reached management where I realized that even the division managers were not completely clear on what the mission was. They did not see the whole picture!

During the outdoor activity, it became crystal clear that each one was involved in their own small world, at best within their own division. Actually, we realized that it had even reached an absurd level of non-economic competition for the organization. For example, divisions poaching clients from each other.

This unreasonable conduct of the employees was in fact a symptom, which reinforced the understanding that the problem began with management who, instead of working as one synergic management, worked as separate groups of VPs. This is a common issue in many organizations because the VP's performance is evaluated by their own division, which is the only thing that counts when coming to work every morning. On the other hand, it goes without saying that you cannot manage a company without a supportive and uniformed strategy even when it demands occasional, on the spot, local concessions.

It is Just Me, My Crate and I!

Since the issue of separate intra-organizational conduct is so broad and complex, I will allow myself to expand on it a little, because the detection, assessment, and handling of it can shortens many processes.

"It is outrageous that I send a truck at four in the afternoon to a customer who is buying two crates of produce and it does not even cover the truck's ride!" This was a permanent complaint by the distribution manager at a company I worked for. This caused a reaction, apparently a permanent one, from the sales manager in the organization who exclaimed – "Do you want me to lose a customer over two crates I don't send him?"

Indeed, there is a big question here that begins with a query – in our company, are we even aware that we are paying for transport? The sales manager was aware, for example, but he also knew that it was not part of his evaluation. In other words, his immediate need to serve his independent goals outweighed the overall strategic vision. This showed just how important it was to raise this question for discussion at the highest level of the company – to check if there is a loss of business due to this dilemma.

I came across another more extreme example of this narrow-minded outlook whereby employees' career paths were being delayed. It goes more or less like this – a high-performing employee wants to apply for a vacant position in another division, but the manager torpedoes it, because they do not want to lose this employee. Where does this stand in the overall vision of the company?

Upon the discovery of such a torpedo in one of the companies, the CEO conveyed an explicit directive that at no cost will any employee's promotion be blocked. The interest of promoting employees comes before the narrow divisional benefit. This is correct from the business aspect and as a message in the cultural-organizational aspect, because if employees have the potential to advance – but not with you – there is a good chance they will just wave you goodbye and leave for another company. Then what have we gained?

In cases like these, we cannot ignore the message being sent down the chain – there is a glass ceiling, even for the best employees! It is absurd but it happens all the time and sometimes in a less direct manner. If your boss gives a sour reaction to anyone who wants to be promoted to another division, it is enough for you not to want to run for another position.

Obviously, this leaves you with two options: to leave – or stay – both leaving one feeling disgruntled. This way both you and the organization lose out. In addition, you need to remember that this behavior spreads at unbelievable speed. The internal communication of such messages runs lengthwise and widthwise in seconds.

"No matter how good or successful you are or how clever or crafty, your business and its future are in the hands of the people you hire"

Akio Morita

Excuse Me, Which One of You is Entitled to a Bonus?

The question to ask is why people stay in their own small circle. The answer is that if I, as an employee, no matter what level, keep hearing in the overt messages and in those below the surface, that I should just get on with my job and not bother anyone or anything, then I am clearly going to be in that kind of mindset. You, as manager, cannot come afterwards and say to me something like – 'Listen, you do not seem to be helping out your colleague from the other division or even your colleague sitting next to you and that is harming things...'

The automatic response to the above would be along the line of – 'Excuse me, what do you want from me? Do you listen when I have something to say? Do you include me? So, how come you are demanding that I step out of my little box that you pushed me into?' The employee would be right, because everything is connected and dependent on everything, and as an assessor, someone who is supposed to solve problems, you need to remember this.

The first step in handling the cases I encountered of non-uniformed policy issues was to set goals for the whole chain of management. For example, I always insist that the threshold conditions for a bonus at the VP level is dependent upon the company being profitable or not. It may be that one of the VPs exceeded his or her target, but the company did not. In my opinion, it does not make sense for the VP to be rewarded, as he or she is part of management, and therefore should have an overall interest. Obviously if this VP does not internalize the systemic approach, there is no way that the message will trickle down to the lower levels and this is very dangerous – for the VP as well!

In my experience, in order for the message to be absorbed, it has to go through the VP and, vice-versa – if the senior manager internalizes the message, it will be spread easily and efficiently.

Let us take, for example, a company that has four or

five substantial divisions, of which one or two meet their goals just fine, but the other three are bringing the company down.

If the company gets into trouble or does not meet its goals, the distinction between the divisions will be over. No one is going to say – 'The problem is just with X, so we'll work to solve only that.' Of course not! The crisis will belong to the whole organization. Therefore, it is so important for the employees to understand that adopting the general strategic approach is in the personal interest of each and every one of them.

Sometimes people internalize things better if they have set goals, but I think that here, as well, it would be more effective to connect everyone through emotion and not with the 'carrot and stick' approach. This is a process of culture and assimilation.

Going back to the case we presented above regarding the split management – after we discovered the problems in the lower levels, that they had originated somewhere along the chain of the higher ranks, we simultaneously conducted intensive activities on how to work in headquarters, including structured workshops for senior management, together with division managers. The aim was to instill the language and to ingrain the new culture of conduct. From there, we went down one level to the department managers and then to the team leaders. In other words, in such a case it is worthwhile to reconstruct the whole procedure of conduct, methodology, language and rules.

In any case, the real bonus to having an organizational perception with an overall interest is a better connection between all those concerned. Just like in a circle – this connection will make everyone feel they have an impact, become more involved and therefore, be more open to accepting the concept of 'togetherness' and sharing the same destiny.

> *"Keep your eyes on the stars,*
> *and your feet on the ground"*
>
> **Theodore Roosevelt**

Outdoor Events
SMART GAMES
(The Fourth Stage of the Model)

After we have done what is called 'the pen and paper assessment' (yes, I am aware of the fact that it has been a while since it has actually been a piece of paper and an actual pen, but that is the way it is with names...) I recommend going for a direct and natural extension – which is outdoor events

These events take place outside of the organizational space and are recognized as being experiential. They are intended for workers and managers, with the emphasis on developing teamwork in field conditions, examining guidance and leadership skills, testing time management skills and, of course, offer great potential for team building.

The events simulate situations in the form of games, and if you know what to look for, you can obtain a lot of important information from watching them. In fact, if you follow the steps in the model and arrive at the outdoor events focused, thanks to the mapping process – knowing what to look for and which areas should get special attention – you will receive relatively quick insights using this tool.

These games can also be a structured observation for evaluation centers at the highest possible level, except that in this case it is not just about identifying individuals and their capabilities, but about assessments that indicate the behavior of the teams, the groups, the departments, and the interactions between them.

The outdoor events are considered to be a supportive tool, more practical than theoretical, in which the tasks you create allow examination from several angles – from the level of thinking to the strategic capabilities on to the planning and negotiating between the teams. Thus, if you build the process properly, you have all the elements found in the organization. Although you are simulating them in the form of a game, in practice it reflects almost precisely the happenings in the workplace.

Therefore, when asked how I define an event, I think about it as a process that is affected by reality, and less as something I think or know, or assume to know, how they are done. You get the whole picture at once – alive, real, without beautifications and without cutting corners. All you need to know is – how to read it!

Two Minutes and the Show will be Over!

We know, and we are reminded once again, that in the first few minutes of a game, people are still putting on a show, but very quickly they get into the competition and behave normally, which allows for the array of forces to be identified in a limited, constricted, and defined time.

Within minutes, you will notice those employees who sit on the fence, take less initiative and are less involved, and of course, you will immediately see the stars as well. Many times, an employee who, during stages one and two of the 'pen and paper assessment' had been pushed to the end of the scale, stands out as a natural leader, initiator, and front-runner during the outdoor activities.

At this stage, to be effective you should take note of who is who. This is usually apparent during teamwork, in which there are also elements of individual exercises, which form a small group that grows as the game continues. The next step is to take the whole system and examine synergies and tasks that require collaboration. This is where you will notice, for example, how much trust and confidence there is between the group members; whether the employees group together in a diversified manner; how much social pressure is exerted in the groups; which employee is more open to negotiation and who understands the overall vision.

In my experience, it is best to construct the process gradually – beginning with the team, then moving on to the department, the wing and then the division. Doing it gradually prevents too big an onslaught in a task at the level of division, in which smaller teams may get lost and employees, whom you wish to pinpoint, fade into the background.

The correct construction of the process is required in advance of course. This includes carefully preparing the HR personnel with forms detailing what needs to be observed and what is important to be addressed. I also try to bring in professionals from the field of psychology, who specialize in assessments, providing additional skilled reinforcements.

The objective is always that the team observing, which as mentioned above consists of HR personnel, from managers to external professionals, will be as open and as unbiased as possible. That is also the reason why I do not present my assessment analyses to the observers. I try my best for them to come as '*tabula rasa*', free of influences and biases, especially towards the employees, which also include the different units.

Obviously, you are required to guide and direct the observers as to what to pay attention to and how to rank everything. It is important for everyone to understand the orientation of the organization and the structure you hope to eventually examine.

If anybody is wondering why the need for so many evaluators – theoretical and practical, experience has proven repeatedly that the more evaluators there are, the more accurate, reliable, and sharp the results end up being.

Personal Invites, Stimulate the System

We have mentioned above the initial apprehension of the employees, which sometimes is so extensive it is even evident during the outdoor activities – which is basically considered a treat for them. Even on a two-day outing in which you do your best to indulge them and make them feel as good as possible, you will still hear those whispering from the sidelines – 'I wonder what the catch is' or 'What streamlining process are they cooking up for us.' This also stems from the fact that employees are not used to employers investing in them. There is something twisted in this understanding, but it is not their fault. This is how they are used to being managed. Therefore, you need to come from a good, transparent, and genuine place, with clean hands – then they will be on your side.

To get the most out of the activities and neutralize the suspicions as much as possible, I tend to do the process in an organized and meticulous manner from all aspects, including those related to marketing.

What does this mean exactly?

I like to aim for the outdoor activities to last two days (by the way, if we really want to activate the desired stress and pressure levels, then the night activity is necessary, because the employees are tired and worn out, so all the protective shells fall away).

I make sure to tease the employees before, to stimulate the system. It begins even with the invitation to the event. Even though today most invitations are digital, I believe that, if it is possible, you should make the effort to invest in printed invitations, because they create a one-of-a-kind effect. I definitely make an effort here for the invitation to include a booklet explaining what the outdoor activities are – what are the goals and what we would like to achieve. The booklet should provide the location, what they need to bring, and include an agenda. All this information will make it clear to them what processes they will undergo. This will help calm them down, enabling them to connect with the event.

An employee who receives such an invitation should be able to read between the lines and understand the message it conveys – the company has invested in me; this is not something being done offhandedly, just to be checked off a list.

The first few times I did this, I was severely criticized

by management for printing the invitations. They did not understand why I invested so much into this. Obviously, in this day and age, printed invitations seem completely redundant, but even then, I intuitively felt that it should be done properly, otherwise it becomes trivial, and will catch you on the rebound. I stand by this to this day!

As the years have gone by, I have found this always to be effective. I have seen how the invitations are received by the employees and how amazed they always are. Someone told me that he was sure that outdoor activities were rope games, until he read the article we had sent with the invitation, which explained in details the topics of the activities, about game theory and how to practice it.

One of the responses etched strongly in me was from industrial factory workers. In workplaces like these, I tend to send the invitation to the employees' homes to expose their families to the event. Before and after the event, the workers reactions very from – 'Wow, my kids jumped on top of me and asked if I was going to take a course' or 'You know, I have been here for 30 years, I have never been treated like this or been spoken to and until now, I have never been taken anywhere.' 'My wife did not stop flipping through the invitation and exclaiming how wonderful it is! It was so carefully planned, and she could not believe there was no hidden agenda.'

It is all Thanks to the Hidden Watermelons!

During the activities, you should also provide the employees with small indulgences, to make them feel that you have really thought of everything. Just take for example portable toilets – there is always the option to just bring the cheapest ones and be done with it.

But no!

I strive to bring the fanciest portable toilets possible. When the employees go to their rooms in the afternoon to freshen up and change clothes, there is always some activity-related treat waiting for them on their pillows. An example for going the extra mile – part of an activity we did was a treasure hunt in one of the local rivers. We hid watermelons inside the bushes and the water, which caused great excitement when they were found. Also, make an effort on the 'how'!

I have found that with all the benefits in bringing treats, in the end they also do not entail that much spending. So, if you have already made up your mind to invest, remember that something that may seem so small can go a long way! It has an impact on the way the employees relate to the activity, their gratitude and makes them feel they are being taken seriously and therefore, feel obligated to invest themselves.

Naturally on the last day of outdoor activities all management joins in and everyone listens together to the conclusions. This is the last piece of evidence that the event is of great importance because, if management has come, something substantial must be going on.

The activities are conducted in integrated groups, some from here and others from there – a mixture from different divisions and departments, because the work in the organization cannot come to a complete stop, and there is also much benefit to be had from the integrated groups. After all outdoor activities, I receive calls from the employees' managers asking – 'What did you do to them? They are so excited and smiling constantly. What exactly happened there?'

In my eyes, this is worth a lot! In fact, the outcome does not have a monetary price, which sometimes makes it difficult to explain to managers and management. There will always be those that complain and say – 'You are going to invest money and what exactly will come out of it?'

No matter how much you try, it is difficult to describe the crucial and lasting impact of the outdoor activities.

Outdoor Events as Part of the
Mapping Process, Changes in Motion

Outdoor events are a tool used for many purposes, but in our context, I think they provide a different angle to the mapping process. They produce benefits for this process, and along the way, prepare the infrastructure for implementation, collaboration and creating a new organizational spirit.

In addition to the insights revealed during the activities, they can also corroborate and confirm what we already know and can sometimes correct information from the earlier stages of the assessments if they turn out to be incorrect or inaccurate.

If we survey the path of the Mapping process described here, starting with the initial process of meeting with employees and joining meetings, and then moving on to the in-depth assessment with the teams, together with the outdoor activity assessment, we find we are connecting people and touching their lives. In other words, throughout this whole experience, a new culture is instilled without having to wait until the process has been completed theoretically by the higher levels, and only then beginning to apply it. During the mentioned process, you have already begun to plant the seeds of collaboration, of making direct contact and placing the employees at center stage. These issues greatly serve the balance we so long for.

As we have seen here, in each stage of the mapping and assessment process, it is essential that the HR manager takes a step back and becomes the observer assessing from the sideline. It is true you are a colleague, but now it is necessary for you to grasp the many details that make up the big picture.

I wish to repeat this essential point, because if you get the mapping and assessment stage wrong, then your point of view will be twisted. Therefore, this crucial and dramatic stage needs to be worked on with a lot of patience, with as many methods and meetings as possible and with a diverse range of employees.

Expanding the circles will help you identify the essential points, to see how they affect and are affected by one another. For example, if you work in an organization in which it is unclear what the level of interaction and dialogue is between the workers, this point needs to be emphasized on all levels. Obviously if it manifests itself in the personal discussions, roundtable discussions and the different management meetings, it should narrow down your range and indicate that it is most probably a key issue – which needs to be analyzed and dealt with as such.

CHAPTER 4

The Seesaw of Organizational Powers

Assessment Follow-Up Processes

(THE FIFTH STAGE OF THE MODEL)

"People will forget what you said, people will forget what you did, but people will never forget how you made them feel"
Maya Angelou

In this stage of the model, we deal with processes that follow-up on the assessment stage and the work plans. In other words, the different aspects of the practical work. Among other things, we will examine:

- When is the right time to take a step back?
- Why is it necessary for previous work plans to be taken into consideration?
- How do we work around prejudice?
- How much can inflated egos deceive?
- How to develop plans for employee development and organizational excellence in light of the findings from the previous stages?

Allow me to quote the great and brilliant Lee Iacocca who said – *"The ability to concentrate and to use your time well is everything"* and apply this quote to the mapping process as well. In other words, here we have described a process, which, although relatively short in duration, is solid, intensive, and focused. It needs to be dealt with in conjunction with work plans and formed strategies.

In my opinion, at every stage, both during and after the mapping processes, the questions to be asked are – 'What are the effects of these actions we have taken? What are the results? Are we headed in the right direction?' There is no need to feel embarrassed if changes need to be made while going through the process.

If some actions that are initiated do not hit the mark and do not cause the expected results – maybe even having the opposite effect – then be flexible! You will be evaluated for your ability to map out and juggle situations in many directions. The most important thing is to be attentive.

For that reason, even when I enter the third stage – the analysis – described above, I will continue with assessments. Of course, I do not go through the whole process again, but I continue to hold meetings with employees from all levels, including roundtable discussions. I continue to sit in on meetings, go on field trips – learning constantly. Basically, this needs to be treated as a period of learning – even though the assessments have already been checked and internalized, they now must be targeted for analysis. It is worthwhile not letting up, because one of the following may occur – either you will come across new things you had not noticed before, or you will reinforce what you already know, or both simultaneously. In any case, these are important matters, connecting well with the perception of the open door and 'talking organization' policies, which I strongly believe should be a part of the culture of conduct, regardless of the mapping process.

In my opinion, it is a matter of principle, which applies to managers at all levels and specifically to HR, to aim for allowing employees to express their opinions and to be listened to. After all, sitting in an office in the ivory tower prevents the upper levels from understanding what is happening in the organization. Of course, it is possible to open all the theoretical books and debate from sunrise to sunset, providing excellent presentations that will sound good and look even greater – but the only disadvantage is that nothing will change. Or to be exact, changes might happen that you would really rather prevent – like cynicism coming from the field.

I will be cautious in adding that it is not as if you only have one shot... But it is pretty close to that. That is why it is so important to understand how the process is initiated. If you fail to really touch on the pressing issues, trying to repair it afterwards will be much harder!

Presenting the Mapping Process, Do Not Cut Corners!

I would like to dwell for a moment on presenting the mapping findings required of you as HR manager. This is a critical stage, especially when presenting management with the less desirable findings, and I recommend presenting things as they are. The trick is to find a polite, respectable, and explanatory way to do it without cutting corners. You must remember – among other things – you are being tested here!

One needs to take into consideration that the need for caution stems from the fact that you might cause too much of a shock in the organization; therefore, you need to be aware of, and attentive to, all the fluctuations in the different levels throughout the whole process. Especially since, although you set out to improve matters, you might have created a crisis instead with intensities you could not have imagined. Therefore, changes need to be made carefully, with patience and transparency, and the more your partners are involved in the process from its early stages, the more connected they will be in the end.

Presenting the mapping needs to be a direct continuation of the main motto that we are trying to convey in all directions and at each level and it concerns the need to touch people emotionally. When your intentions are sincere, with no pretense or hidden interests, but just by stating facts as they are, even if sometimes they are unpleasant – you have a good chance of succeeding!

It is No Picnic! There is no sugarcoating it. Situations in which 'tough love' is needed are never a picnic. It is not pleasant to sit with the managers and tell them – 'You have raised a long list of issues here, and I am sorry to tell you that you are responsible for some of them. As I have already stated, it is easy to aim upwards. Let us look downwards for a moment. How do you treat your employees? Are you not practicing the very same patterns against which you preach?'

In any case, it is difficult coming into an organization and exposing the roadmap that they have been following until now. There is no other choice though. This is an essential stage from which to start the activities for improvement.

Feedback as a Tool and the Illusions of Workshops

Examining the frequency of meetings between all levels of management is an important factor that I focus on in particular, because from that I can deduce whether the organization advocates the open door policy, and whether it listens and learns. It turns out that you can find in certain organizations employees who have been there for years and who have seen the CEO one time, by chance, in the elevator. Alternatively, there are organizations in which the CEOs' presence is constantly felt. They go into the field, conduct roundtable discussions, and set up random meetings with employees. Obviously, there is a whole range in the middle. In principle, the essence of these companies is completely different from one another and should therefore be treated accordingly.

One of the best indicators for examining the level of internal dialogue in the organization is feedback. It is an excellent tool, which, in my opinion, should be used at least once a year and if necessary, even once every three months. I see it as a great advantage because it is unmediated dialogue between the employee and the manager, and the only question in this regard should be – what is the correct frequency of feedback for the organization?

In 'open' companies, where there are ongoing discussions and therefore not requiring procedures and forms to be filled out, the feedback process can be applied once a year. It is necessary only to assess the situation and analyze directions and trends.

In many places, I have encountered the sad fact that the feedback process is, in reality, the only meeting taking place between employees and their managers. Having no other interaction makes the process very technical – 'Here you are doing a good job. Here you need to improve.' It comes across with less warmth, less personal interaction and without any emotion – which is a pity.

During the actual assessment, I tend to count less on

feedback solely from the managers' evaluations. However, when I find feedback reports from beforehand – those, I definitely study. Since I perceive the feedback process to be a substantial part of conducting dialogue with the employee, I will definitely retrieve as much information as possible from past processes.

> *"Where is the knowledge*
> *we have lost in information?"*
>
> **T.S. Eliot**

It is Worthwhile Investigating What Happened Before You!

In general, when you come to an organization that has a history of procedures, you need to examine what is happening, what the trends are and what are the general directions. I, for one, go over all the work plans related to the field of development and human capital of at least a few years back, to get an idea where I have landed. There have been cases in which I have found past attempts doing the activities that I was now supposed to lead. This is where I dive in deep to understand what went wrong.

After all, it is obvious that in most organizations you will find at least attempts at development. There are always workshops and courses, enrichments, and training. The question is what was their basis?

Let us presume excellent training sessions were

undertaken, but none of the managers showed any interest in finding out how they went when their workers returned – here you get the opposite effect. If the employee, returning from a training session, is asked to prepare a presentation for the team or the department showing what they learned, you will receive positive effects in a flash. Not only will it show that you are supportive and caring, but their knowledge will be used for the benefit of the whole company, allowing personal growth for the organization. In other words, something small and basic that happens in every company can be wrapped differently and with a better infrastructure benefitting everyone.

Therefore, the work, training, and development plans that were undertaken before your time in the organization, are foundations that need to be explored, to learn how they were used, and to see how it may affect the way you work, sometimes even finding some use for those plans.

I discovered another interesting fact about previous training plans, which should be examined at the assessment stage – sometimes these plans, through no fault of their own, become some kind of fringe benefit. The ability to compensate employees, especially in large companies, is limited and the lower you go down the ranks, the less chance you have of giving employees a bonus. So sometimes employees chosen for having excelled in their division are sent to some kind of training just so 'they do not say we don't do anything for them.' It is impossible to be fake in these situations, because if employees sent to a course find that upon return no one has shown any interest in what they have experienced, they will get the drift very quickly – the course was just a diversion, a manager's obligation. There are many companies in which you find that the training is conducted simply to check them off a list.

But what is gained in the end?

You realize that the desired results are not obtained even in places where a lot of money has been invested. For example – in a new position I began, I found that in the company there had been activities for the employees' welfare and development, which had achieved exclamations of approval from the employees – the best courses and most invested activities! However, from a more in-depth look, it was evident that these courses were not people-oriented but activity-oriented. There were, for example, courses provided by the most exclusive companies in the market, training held overseas, international exhibitions etc. When I spoke with employees who had returned from one of these exhibitions, they said how amazing it was from a professional aspect, but how much of a letdown it was in terms of the silence that followed.

When I send managers and employees to international conferences, they are required to return with organized input, to be presented and implemented in every relevant area in the company. I sit with them to understand in detail what they experienced there, what they learned, what we can instill going forward, etc. In other words – it gives the activity significance from an organizational aspect and not just from an individual one. The employees are aware beforehand that they are going not only as individuals, but as representatives of the company as well. If they had fun doing it, great – but that is not the main goal.

Where Did All the Managers Go?

There is no doubting the fact that HR managers need to work through the organization to learn all about it. For me, this realization was reinforced when I was appointed VP for the first time, and I arrived at a company conference. There were about 20 HR managers on my team and we were all sitting in the conference, where the point was to discuss the business and financial goals and results.

Those present were first level managers below VPs, and each of the 20 were HR managers of either a division or a subsidiary. We all had high– ranking roles. We were all present in the conference, until the CFO stood up to give a lecture about the financial reports. To my shock, I saw that as he came on stage all my managers got up to leave.

When I stepped out to ask them what was going on, they replied that since the CFO was going to present the financial reports, which did not interest them, they felt free to leave. I did not utter a word and just went back inside, but I realized that there was a serious issue with perception. After all, we were not some nonprofit association or a youth movement – we were a company operating a business. If the HR managers did not comprehend that they needed to take a major interest in the financial reports and in how the company is going to profit – then we were in trouble.

Moreover, not only were they required to check in which areas the company was earning and in which they were not and go back and analyze areas in need of improvement – but some of the business solutions were in their hands. For example, if the reports show that there is a burning issue in sales, maybe there is a need to consider investing in programs of compensation for employees there, in trainings and tools that will help them.

Since the departure of those managers from that conference, I have insisted that we, too, as HR, need to build work plans not only in the division itself – as is usually created with clear measurements based on familiarity or assessments – but only after we have understood the company's work policy.

In other stern words – without the organization's business plan, I do not build plans of action for HR. I request that every clause in the business plan is translated into what it means for HR, because if we create something that does not support the business goal – then why do it?

Prejudice
Have You Checked Down Below as Well?

The biggest challenge lurking in assessments is drawing hasty conclusions from what is visible on the surface. Many times, these are incorrect inferences, stemming from the fact that we come into an organization and generally take the managers' words as a gospel. The result – our whole outlook is affected by their points of view

This is a fundamental mistake that often leads to the formation of an incorrect plan of action. From all the stages in the mapping and assessment listed here, it is clear that this would be a mistake in many aspects – the main one being the managers' prejudice.

That same biased opinion is the reason I refrain from recommending any particular working model, because I have found that most of them rely too much on the managers' evaluations, which may actually be part of the problems we are trying to assess.

Let us take for example the regular templates whose starting point is to map out high-performance employees to supposedly understand who needs to be compensated and who needs to be retained. Let us think about this for a moment – who decides on the initial classification? It is built upon the managers' statements and perceptions regarding their subordinates, and I am not so sure that the managers are 'interest-free'. They are definitely not free of emotions – we are all human beings! So, it is alright to work based on a certain model, but this cannot be the only factor, and the fact that there may be prejudice should definitely be kept in mind.

Floating on Pink Clouds

Another example for bias, is an argument I had in one of the organizations about the bonus for outstanding employees, which was based entirely on the managers' evaluations and rankings (again, not objectively) of their subordinates. My claim was that, since diligent employees should be role models in their environments, a parameter of what their colleagues think of them should be included. The reply was – 'What for? What is there for them to say?' To which I responded – 'A lot! They know them from up close. They cannot hide anything from their colleagues.'

After checking the diligent candidates from the three previous years, we found that it was always the same circle from which the same employees were selected, each time in different order. When we entered their colleagues' ranking in a sociometric questionnaire, we found candidates who had never been selected, and many of the employees who had been selected before, were taken off the lists.

Of course, this example is not to claim that managers' evaluations carry no weight and that they do not know their employees, but it comes to remind us of the whole truth and not just part of it – we are all mere mortals!

Irrelevant matters influence us and that is fine, but it needs to be factored into the assessments for mapping or deciding on promotions or bonuses. Therefore, it is best to include emotion-free and less biased elements.

Bias can also be amazing on the other side of the coin. Here is another example I encountered when I came to do a mapping process in a large organization. I began summoning employees to one-on-one discussions with me. It all seemed to be going too well and I felt as if I was being enveloped in a pink cloud, with world champions all rooting for each other. It was one rosy personal discussion after another. Everyone was happy – everything was perfect!

After a few discussions, I asked the secretary who was deciding which employee to call in, and she told me that she was doing it in coordination with the VP's secretary. Together they decided and sent out the invitations. Boom! Everything became clear! From that moment on, the employees were invited randomly, and it turned out that not all was rosy in the organization after all.

"The value of an idea lies in the using of it"

Thomas A. Edison

We Found a Junior Worker in Napoleon's Knapsack

On the ride through one's professional life, some stations are less successful while others can be looked at with satisfaction and maybe even with pride. The Atudot **Project3 for discovering and training managers definitely belongs to the second option for me. It took place years ago, but its traces remain to this day**

The project actually began when I decided to initiate the development of a leadership pipeline program in a specific organization. The issue of non-objectivity jumped out at me especially when I wondered how to find candidates. Even though this was my first role as VP, I knew that in this organization their decisions worked the same way – i.e., the high-ranking level employees consult with the managers (some biased) and then they target the employees with the highest potential. I decided that this time we were going to go about it a different way and I performed a series of tests to discover the less visible and undeveloped talents, which had not yet been revealed. It was a great success, because the tests were unbiased and comprehensive enough and we found excellent employees who otherwise would not have been discovered.

---

3. The Atudot Project received a commendation from the ASTD (American Society for Training & Development)

Goody-Two-Shoes In one of the companies I worked in, I decided to initiate a project for management development and high-potential identification across the entire company – creating a leadership pipeline of 5000 employees.

Since it was a huge organization, I felt that because of its size, complexity and management structure, there was actually no chance for an employee from the lower ranks to stand out and be promoted. This was not only problematic, but also unjust and incorrect. I wanted to try to see how things could be done differently.

I began to learn and read about other projects, and I very quickly reached the understanding that in almost all employees' trainings, the candidates were still being selected in the familiar way – management convenes, consulting here and there, and then marks a backbone of prominent employees known to management. Usually, these are high-performing employees, but still, there is great bias, which we have mentioned already, related to the employee-manager connection.

Let us think for a moment what will happen if we are talking about a goody two-shoes – an employee who does less kicking and behaves according to the norm. It would seem that their chance of being targeted for the pipeline should increase – no?

I, for one, who throughout my own personal path was considered quite a rebel, although not particularly insolent (alright, maybe a little), think that there are worse things than someone who does not automatically nod and agree to everything, always making out as if all is peachy. An employee, who is constantly satisfied and always ready to please, will repeatedly continue to do the same thing, receiving the same results. So what is the point?

Looking for THE Soldier In my opinion, when we talk about creating a leadership pipeline, we want to see the opposite – a more independent thinker, someone who has a backbone, even if somewhat rebellious. I am not talking about undermining authority, but something more basic – not taking things at face value.

In the surveys I conducted, I found to my surprise that in most of the companies, including large banks, giant organizations and even leading hi-tech companies, employee selection is indeed done with the managers. I decided that this time we were not going to repeat the same old story.

My assumption was that in a company with thousands of employees, it is almost impossible for an outstanding employee not to be overlooked because of the method of selection. It is illogical! Even statistically, it is impossible. It was obvious that in the higher levels – those that are more exposed and familiar – the employees would be easier to locate. But, what about the less visible places where the more basic work takes place? Are all the employees there unworthy?

And so, we decided to go on a general hunt throughout the entire organization, accompanied by Napoleon's famous quote – *"Every (French) soldier carries a marshal's baton in his knapsack."*

I really wanted to find that soldier!

Is English a Difficult Language?
Let Us Teach You Then!
After the general direction had been decided, with the full backing of the CEO, the following dialogue was held between management and me:

Me: "You know what, let's allow everyone to apply for the pipeline."

Them: "What?! Are you crazy? We have thousands of employees. Can you imagine what would happen here with so many disappointed employees? The whole project will cause more damage than good."

Me: "I understand the concern, but, in my opinion, at the end of the day people are smart. When they see they have been given an opportunity, that the process is transparent, clear and objective and not just some manager's whim and that it actually depends on their own capabilities – there is a good chance that it will work out well."

Them: "Okay, give it a try, even though we are totally skeptical."

We Are Out of the Game! It was obvious that to succeed we needed a system that would classify as best and as 'clean' as possible. I immediately thought of the professionals, the Israeli Air Force, who specialize in this area. They have the desired classification methods. And so, we found three psychologists who had worked for years with the best pilots, and we recruited them for the task.

Luckily for us, they were enthusiastic and open to the challenge. They were also familiar with the world of employee development and therefore understood that this time we were trying something innovative. They had the patience and the understanding that was required for long hours of preparation during meetings with us to make accurate adjustments as possible to what we were looking for.

In the beginning, we decided together that we had to create a minimal level of capabilities, and when we investigated more deeply, we reached the conclusion that, beyond these capabilities, nothing else was required – not even a BA nor a matriculation certificate.

We worked on two courses – one for employees with minimum qualifications and the other for engineers and other academics, with a professional but not a managerial background. In both tracks, we wanted the tests to identify inner strengths and capabilities, as minimal as they may be, such as leadership, motivating people and ambition.

At this point, the question arose of what to do if an employee is talented and suitable but had never learned English and did not know how to speak the language. We decided that if that was the only obstacle, we would send them to learn English at our expense and a year after that they would be back on track to be re-chosen. We did not want to strike down those who did not meet our standards, but rather to embrace them.

The second important decision we made was that, if any employees did not pass the tests, they would have a private session with a psychologist, in which they would receive organized and professional feedback, detailing where their strengths lie, what their weaknesses were and in what areas they needed support. We, for our part, were attentive and extended any assistance required for both training and reinforcements, which created additional confidence in the process.

We decided that the managers could give their opinions as part of the classification process; however, their opinions would not count as the casting vote but rather carry some weight in the final decision. As HR managers, we took ourselves out of the equation knowing that we were forbidden to get involved. I informed the examiners that the only bar I was setting was the number of employees. All the rest was on them.

> *"The biggest risk is not taking any risk"*
> **Mark Zuckerberg**

Is it Too Risky? Well, It Must Be Done!

Up until now, everything sounds hunky-dory, but the truth is that I had butterflies in my stomach. I remember that during the time that the project was being initiated, I participated in a workshop, with my deputy, about leadership pipeline and management development. They presented a very impressive project from one of the banks that had constructed an excellent program for a leadership pipeline, but here as well, it was the managers who targeted the 30 employees and went with them.

When I asked them why they did not open the opportunity to more employees, they replied that they thought of allowing employees from one level down to participate. I said to them – "No, no. Why did you not open it up to the whole company?" The lecturer went pale and replied – "Listen, that is unacceptable. It is not something that is done anywhere. It is too dangerous. This is a huge investment of money and energy, and, in the end, how many employees will actually be selected?"

At that moment I said to myself – Okay, this is exactly what needs to be done!

If I had any concerns or hesitations before then, her reply made it distinctly clear to me that I was moving in the right direction.

What Does it Say About Me? As the preparations progressed and the noise level in the company increased, even the most skeptical managers began to understand what was really going on. In the beginning of the process the entire managerial system, especially at the level of the units, did not see the project as substantial, and their feedback was mainly full of cynicism and skepticism. As soon as they realized that in meetings, management were presenting the data on how many candidates there were, how many were accepted and where from – it began to immediately trickle down to the unit managers. Those who had underestimated the project began to feel isolated when they realized that the number of candidates from their team was a reflection on them.

All of a sudden, when there were rumors about one division having 20 candidates and another having none, the division managers realized that this did not show them in a favorable light. From that point on, managers began to push their employees with questions like

– 'Why are you not participating? Go ahead, sign up! What do you have to lose?'

A competition – open and covert – began around which manager was sending more employees. It turned the organization upside down, lit a fire around the subject, and every time an employee returned from a test or assessment, their managers wanted to know every detail, mainly because it was their reputation on the line. We had not anticipated nor planned for it to happen so early on. I had predicted that a competition would develop, but not with such intensity. I had assumed it would come after the classifications.

I was wrong! It already started at the registration stage.

We Are Still Looking for Mr. Complaint!

We were on our way! There were more than 400 applicants, when we were expecting a lot less. Ten percent of them began the actual process. It was crazy! There was not a single applicant, not one, who complained. This was a great surprise, since we were certain that there is always someone who complains – not here!

On the contrary – a discussion started in the organization along the lines of – 'I don't know English and they are now sending me to a course at their expense!' Or – 'Wow, I had a meeting with the psychologists, and they mapped out stuff for me. I now understand what I need to do, what I am good at and what I need to work on.' Basically, between the lines they were saying – 'They obviously really mean what they say and want to see us being promoted.'

It was obvious to all, that the mapping process was completely transparent and without any intervention from us, which lowered the anxiety level considerably. What also became obvious to the employees, was our interest and caring and I think the greatest impact was finding many employees with tremendous potential.

I remember one of them in particular.

Reading between the Lines Do you remember the example of the marshal's baton in Napoleon's knapsack? Well, we did not find the soldier, but we found an employee we would have never otherwise discovered.

He had a very low-ranking position. He was extremely intelligent and had just finished his military service. He was a newlywed and in dire need of money. He worked really hard, especially at nights, and was making a nice living. Obviously, none of the managers 'saw' him. His work was mainly outdoors, so he hardly interacted with the other employees.

His manager signed him up for the tests and he passed them in the top 20 percent in the general distribution. During his training, we sent him to study for a BA and, before he had even finished his degree, he was appointed team leader. By the end of the training, he was already managing a department and one year later, he was in charge of a central warehouse and studying for his MA.

Our training course included academia as well as workshops. We collaborated with one of the leading colleges in Israel and together, once a year, we built a management course on two different levels – for academics and non-academics. Our partners in the college were very connected to the idea and cooperated closely. We invested in an organized and serious trip overseas, with the participants preparing assignments for before and after. Included, were many pre-workshops, lectures, seminars, learning from other organizations, and complex processes.

An Explosive Time Abroad!

We decided to do the training differently outside of Israel as well. For example, we found a school in The Netherlands that deals with firefighting and rescue, and the simulation of real-life situations. In other words, real fire is lit and then the cadets practice rescues from burning airplanes, buildings, buses and more. They really take it to extremes! We thought this would be a good start to show how far training can go.

So, instead of more theoretical explanations, they took 40 of us, laid us down on our backs in a special container with all the relevant gear, and set off an explosion of oxygen overhead. After that, we had to enter a building in which there was zero visibility due to the heavy smoke and they taught us how to follow one another. It was really an out-of-this-world experience.

Following the above, we decided to take advantage of our stay in The Netherlands to learn about order, control, and monitoring so for the sake of illustration, we went to a port in Rotterdam to see how the world of shipping containers and loading works there. It was a very significant and impressive visit, especially since we were introduced to a world of complexity, too difficult to describe, where precision counts for every moment and every moment is measured in monetary terms. Being European, these matters are taken very seriously, and before the visit, they sent us presentations and preliminary explanations. Our delegation came very prepared, proficient in all the material and armed with plenty of questions.

Do You Have a Manager on You Perhaps?

The whole training process, lasting about a year, yielded excellent results, not only for the participants themselves, but also for the employees who applied and were not accepted. The fact that you applied for the leadership pipeline already puts you in a different place in terms of your self-image and the way the company perceives you. It marks you as an employee with ambition, a willingness to deal and a desire to become a manager. Not only does it boost your ego as an employee, but it does wonders for your peers as well.

During the course, we made sure that only employees from the pipeline would be considered for any position that became available, and this hit the mark repeatedly. More than 30 percent of the employees from the pipeline were promoted before they had even finished their training course, because we had all the information we needed about them — we knew their capabilities and their potential.

The real proof of success I got was when I began to receive phone calls, not just from the company but from subsidiaries as well, requesting to take on graduates of the program. That was the highlight for me. Looking back today, I can say with certainty that the vast majority of the senior management in that same organization came out of the program.

A Crazy Gamble! In retrospect, I say well done to the CEO, who believed in promoting employees and who gave me so much credit, because it was a crazy gamble. At that point, I was only at the beginning of my path so I could have very easily failed. Was I too inexperienced to have calculated the risk? Probably. Would I do it all over again? Probably. Absolutely!

MANAGERS, EMPLOYEES AND IN-BETWEENS

At some stage, we have all encountered management ailments – excessive forcefulness, inflated egos and bosses who live in fantasyland

Charisma Saves Words I would like to revert to the issue of listening and the emphasis I put on it during the mapping process, as well as its importance in the post-mapping process and in general – and from there to discuss managers who are unable to remain silent and focus on what someone else has to say.

I practice focused listening all the time, with ever-changing intensities and within all levels of an organization – in management meetings, department meetings, team meetings etc. Anyone who is wondering if a manager's status is harmed by being the silent listener, I can share from my own experience – at the end of the day, it does not matter what you actually say. As a manager, if you have charisma and a presence, even if you do not utter a word, it will be impossible to ignore you. So, do not try to sell something you do not actually have, and most importantly remember to always come from a place of humility. Leave your ego behind.

"Awareness and ego cannot co-exist"

Eckhart Tolle

The Ego Has A Will of Its Own!

This is a good opportunity to write a couple of words about that same ego – the one that Freud called the central part of the human consciousness; it exists in each and every one of us. However, I have yet to see the advantage of an inflated ego in the working world, whereas its harm is visible in almost every company.

I admit that I have an issue with anyone who is driven by their ego. Of course, as human beings, we all have an ego, but when it takes over decision-making and manages us instead of us managing it – we are in trouble.

Inflated egos exist in many organizations, and the higher the rank, the more severe the issue. Unfortunately, I have been in many companies in which the processes of conduct have been affected by it, and the impact is felt in many different ways.

Throughout my professional career, I have encountered CEOs and chairpersons with egos that have made them exceptionally pigheaded. They believed, for example, that they could drive cars worth hundreds of thousands of dollars and then tell their employees that there were going to be fuel cuts. If they had thought logically, and not with their egos, they could have set personal examples and switched to hybrid vehicles, explain the savings, and ask the employees to follow in their footsteps. This could have had a positive influence, but unsurprisingly, there was a major outburst instead.

Another example of inflated egos are managers being extremely uncooperative with their employees. Sometimes it can be so extreme that when I asked the VPs why they were not engaging with their employees, they would reply – 'Why should I? Why do I need to engage with them? Why should I have anything to do with them?' Sometimes there is no actual way to explain to them how much damage they are causing, and they are unable to grasp the known fact – when you give, you get back twofold.

Step Out of Your Bubble! Another phenomenon I have encountered with many VPs when trying to understand how they are feeling and what, in their opinion, is the vibe in the company, is realizing that they are living in a total fantasy world. They are completely disconnected from what is actually happening. It is sometimes to such an extreme that I have met VPs who were convinced they were well liked by their subordinates, unaware that the latter had said terrible things about them. It is incredible to think that inflated egos can allow one to exist in their own impenetrable bubble.

Self-Deception You encounter this phenomenon in initial discussions with managers not revealing what is actually happening, just disclosing what they want you to hear. Some of them actually believe that what they are telling you is real – usually they are the ones with inflated egos. They will say something like – 'I have problems here and there', and only when you examine the situation further, are you able to realize that 'here and there' is actually complete destruction.

I encounter this self-deception too often. One VP, for example, told me in our initial conversation that he and his employees were like family – they were all united and believed in him. Indeed, the employees we met up with repeated this. He ran a division of 400 employees, so it took time to grasp what was actually happening there.

When we began to analyze the situation, we saw that the backbone of his division consisted of employees who had grown with him and who felt an obligation towards him, so they obviously did not challenge him. They even managed to convey this obligation to the level below them, but from the levels further down, it began to fall apart, simply because blind loyalty did not exist there.

Only when I began digging around in these areas did I start to hear contradicting stories. When I entered team meetings, I could tell from the body language and the statements of those present that the tension was palpable. I spoke to the non-committed employees, and I crosschecked information and found a parallel universe to the one the VP was living in.

By Force of Force, Orders, Instructions and Threats

Another common characteristic of managers with large egos is their use of forceful management tools. So, when they are actually required to manage, they do not always have the ability other than to yell out orders, instructions and threats. This becomes their style of management and dictates the atmosphere.

Where is it evident? When does an outburst occur?

When something unusual happens.

I would like to go back to an example I shared before, regarding the volunteer operation we did in a company I was working in and through which we were able to examine the different styles of management. The employees in the organization were asked to help out, on their own free time, in the stores to which we supplied merchandise. Then everything became clear: whose employees came in their largest numbers, and where the strongest opposition came from. It was possible to map out clearly the styles of management and their implications.

Indeed, it is not every day that volunteering is required, but as a boss – someone who just yells out orders, the employees will do as they are told, and not an inch more. Over and above them are the managers who are sometimes unaware that the level below has created a bubble for themselves to which the former have no access. I have encountered cases in which employees and managers formed a social group meeting together after working hours while the manager in charge was completely in the dark. This is definitely a problematic situation on all sides.

"A leader's job is not to put greatness into people, but rather to recognize that it already exists, and to create an environment where that greatness can emerge and grow"

Brad Smith

HUMAN CAPITAL
A FRUITFUL INVESTMENT
(THE SIXTH STAGE OF THE MODEL)

Throughout this whole book, we have constantly reiterated the obvious fact that the significant factor in influencing and promoting companies today – those which are competitive – is human capital. All relative advantages stem from your employees – from your people. So, with this issue being so relevant, with major consensus, how is it possible that in the dozens of board meetings I have attended, I cannot recall even a single meeting in which this topic had actually been discussed?

I am referring to discussions dealing with the development of HR, representing work plans, examining the progress taking place in the business world. In the best-case scenario, a few questions about the welfare activities might arise, ensuring that these activities will not be too costly, because it would be excessive to spend and invest too much here.

Mostly this topic is viewed from a higher level – the focus being on the number of the work force, the cost, how it can be streamlined – all related to the financial aspect. Obviously, I am not disregarding the importance of this aspect. Nevertheless, I have witnessed many discussions about other investments, whether in machinery, equipment, or technology. There have been endless discussions with in-depth, wide analysis, some of them even with external consultants, and hundreds of thousands of dollars have been spent to explore the global market. Getting the job done!

Then I am reminded, once again, that I have never witnessed a discussion about what is obviously the heart of the organization.

What is interesting and misleading about human capital is that the approach to HR has been discussed in Israel and around the world in terms of change, but in reality, I have not yet seen actual movement in these areas over the years.

It is true that one can see a difference in perception – an understanding of the meaning, grasping its importance and the need to care for employees – but it remains to all intents and purposes – a consideration. There are no actual serious discussions about how the company is preparing to cultivate, empower, preserve, promote, and develop the strongest weapons on hand in a world of competition – the people!

If we would compile statistics, which I have not done accurately, I am sure that we would find significant and illogical gaps between the boards of directors' investments in different fields.

How is this paradox explained?

Let us start by stating that the field of human capital is a non-measurable field. It is difficult to quantify the world of development and training. When investing in business processes – either with buying equipment or technology or with improving both – a Return of

Investment (RoI) is conducted. This can be presented, measured in money – even if the calculation is not accurate, at least a number can be attached to the process.

How Can We Calculate
How Much We Have Saved?
In the world of HR, it is difficult to examine the RoI. Let us take, for example, the *Atudot* Project we mentioned earlier regarding management development. Here it was impossible to say in advance – 'We are going to now invest hundreds of thousands of dollars in a small number of employees, but it will definitely be profitable.' It is just impossible to give it a number – how can we translate this into an equation?

In the beginning of the project, all we knew for sure was that we would learn more about the employees. We learned that we could match them with the most accurate and precise jobs and therefore, we would be employing extremely suitable and talented people for management. The force of what really happened as a result of the project was not one that could have been predicted – not the impact that it had on the company, nor on the employees, nor on the atmosphere, nor on the energy it created, nor on the final results – one of which resulted in the creation of a managerial backbone.

Most of the consequences were unpredictable in terms of their positive snowball effect, so that even if we though they might occur, we could not quantify them into money. We can do the calculation retrospectively. How much does recruitment cost for your company? How many failures do you have in external recruitment?

How many managers have been promoted by virtue of their seniority and place in the hierarchy?

Regarding the last query, we have definitely seen on many occasions, examples of employees who were excellent wing managers, being promoted and becoming low-functioning VPs. So, the question to be asked is – who actually determined that they were suitable for the new position? What were the promotion criteria? We all know that employees can find themselves suddenly in a position that is beyond their capabilities, or one they are simply not suited for.

We solved this challenge when we conducted the *Atudot* Project. We conducted comprehensive screenings, which included a wide series of various tests, with a large number of evaluators, and therefore our predications were significantly better. How much did we save?

Did the board of directors understand and support the project when we brought it to the table? Not really, but fortunately the CEO liked it and approved it. And as we know, when a CEO tells a joke, everyone laughs – even if it is not funny – so when they say a project is important – everyone agrees.

Their doubts and nervous giggling could only be heard behind the scenes. When did it all turn around? When did the impact become evident with the employees?

Unfortunately, this project is one example of a small number of others, and certainly does not herald real change yet.

When There Is a Problem, the Slides Come Out

It is true that one can feel a small shift in the

managements of the companies, which is usually dependent on the CEO's attitude. If their agenda entails an
understanding of the importance of the investment – it
has a chance. There are companies, notably in the USA
and particularly the largest ones, but in Israel as well, in
which the CEOs take employee development very seriously and are involved, throughout the whole process, in
the details and application of the plans. It is such a plea-
sure, but these are exceptions to the rule and definitely
do not indicate genuine movement.

When do you find yourself in discussions about
human resources? When there are problems in the working relationships, or when there is a need for streamlining. Then the slides are pulled out in all their glory!

There are no serious meetings conducted in these
forums that discuss what should be done in the company's development plans – how to build up the next generation or the future management backbone. How will
the employees adapt to technological developments?

By the way, the technological statement above can be
a good enough reason for heated discussions with the
board of directors. After all, at the crazy pace in which
things spin today, someone who has just completed a
professional internship, in two years' time will become
irrelevant if they are not continuously retrained. They
may remain knowledgeable in what they have learned,
but in the meantime, the world has moved in different
directions. What do we do about this?

When looking at the level of investment in developing the human capital in the world, usually it is very
high in large companies, with much less in smaller ones

– which, of course, is logical. It is difficult for organizations with a small number of employees to commit their resources.

I was surprised to see that in India – where only just a few years ago they began to realize their ability to become a center for business services in a variety of fields – they have developed the niche of HR quickly and seriously. For that matter, small companies have also joined larger organizations and are constantly conducting seminars and creating updated and relevant information.

I have participated in conferences in Singapore, South Korea and India and, from what I have seen, there is widespread interest and understanding in these places, so much so that sometimes government officials from the Ministries of Education and Employment attend such gatherings.

However, in Israel, as much as it may not appear so on the surface, we are lagging behind – extremely behind.

One of the developments, which is actually causing an acceleration in the process, has to do with the employees' organizations in the workplace and the fact that companies do not know how to deal with them. So, one can supposedly be pleased with this acceleration, but it is coming from the wrong direction. It consists mainly of the companies' unease as to how they should behave with their employees but only out of concern for the workers' unions. Therefore, issues are brought to the center stage only when there is confrontation or when serious streamlining is required.

What I am trying to emphasize here is that discussions about how to deal now with the many demands of workers' organizations, with agreements and confrontations – will not help, because they are coming from a place that does not comprehend the general context and has not prepared any foundations. One needs to remember that this is not something that survives on its own but is something that needs to be nurtured on a regular basis by the development and treatment of employees. It needs to be preemptive!

The Revolution Will Come from the Intermediaries

In my opinion, the conclusion from everything mentioned above is that an actual revolution is required.

How can this be done?

Maybe by allowing the HR personnel to join the board of directors. As far as I know, the majority of these compositions do not include people from these worlds, but only from the world of economics and finance. I believe that if people from the 'soft' worlds, who understand what it means to lead large organizations with broad and practical views, were integrated into such forums, the dialogue would take the necessary turn.

In the end it seems that here too, as in many processes, things will begin to move only when actual steps are taken. In other words, by collaborating with experienced people who have managed HR in large companies, ensuring that they bring it up in the agenda. There is no doubt in my mind that when more and more executive forums receive reports about the investment in human capital, follow the activities, ask for answers and are willing to invest money – a different perspective will be instilled.

In fact, it is not complicated nor sky-high in terms of costs to do moderate activities that are very influential, and we have shown examples of that here too. One thing is for sure – you must have an in-depth understanding of the complexity of the matter and not just deal with areas that are convenient or problematic.

After all, any person of intelligence, understands the importance of HR, but between the understanding and the actual execution, it is easiest and more convenient to just push the matter aside.

Since I think that, at the end of the day, their board of directors guides a company's actual policy, it would be good for us all if they would recognize and internalize these matters. Even a slight change in this forum can cause a revolution.

"Do not go where the path may lead, go instead where there is no path and leave a trail"

Ralph Waldo Emerson

'Everyone Is Human Resources' So Double the Effort!

Every CEO understands that they need a CFO or a VP in marketing. HR? What is that? Everyone is so sure that they understand the field perfectly. As an HR manager, it is more difficult to deal with such stigmas. You have to bring twice as much professionalism and added value and direct them to the company's agendas

I would like to revert to my statements about choosing the recommended models and methods by which to conduct the mapping process. I wrote that I take a little from here and a little from there and tend to use what I have seen work and yield good results. This is after I have sifted through tools, which have proved to be less successful. Only here comes a reservation – a big **BUT**, which is – to have the insight of what works for you in a particular place and time, you need to be exposed to as many models and methods as possible – to learn and expand!

This is how I practice throughout my professional life and of course at this stage of the model as well. I invest my whole being in every subject I touch. I gave one example for this in the *Introduction*, when I wanted to learn more about working relationships. For days, I went to listen to court sessions in Labor Court. Precisely like that! I would arrive in the morning, check to see which sessions were scheduled that day and did my best to enter those that seemed especially complex to me. I would sit in the courtroom with a notebook and take notes.

It became obvious that knowledge in the area of working relationships could not come only from lectures at university, because at the end of the day, if you end up in a courtroom, you need to have read the Labor Constitution and have a full understanding of what is right and wrong. You may then find, however, that a lot depends on who the judge is and what their approach is. I also learned that the judges did not reach decisions quickly, preferring to allow each side to reach a settlement.

What I am repeatedly trying to emphasize is that it does not matter what profession you have chosen and what your rank is, you should study hard and go in as many different directions as possible. You should not accept things blindly, asking as many questions as possible. Then you can add your point of view to the knowledge you acquired – your understanding and your perception. In time, experience, which is very important, will come into play. In the first stage, just come open and ready to absorb and think.

I encounter employees and managers from all levels who want to discuss and hear my opinion about professional matters that are not specifically my expertise. This is great in my eyes! The motto I believe in for everyone, on all levels, is that you should not sit on the fence. Initiate and create your own work plan; build yourself a path for studying; understand what is important for you to see and in which areas it is right for you to be exposed.

Go to the managers and ask questions – this will help you see things in a broader perspective, including in your chosen career path. It does not matter where you end up – what is important is that you are as professional and ready as possible.

In a lecture before 5,000 HR managers, Jack Welch, CEO and chairman of General Electric, was asked what the HR department's job was. He replied that without a doubt the HR manager should be the second most important person in the organization. He continued by saying that from the CEOs point of view, the status of the HR manager should be equal to at least of that of the financial manager. After disclosing these things, there was silence in the hall. Surprised by the silence, he asked if it is not the same in other companies and requested that anyone who works in a company, in which the CEO respects the HR manager on the same level as the financial manager, should raise their hand.

Fifty out of the 5,000 hands were raised[4].

4. Taken from the book: Winning: The Answers by Jack and Suzy Welch.

Who Said 'Overtime'?

Today, especially in the world of HR, there are vast amounts of models, theories and research, some complementing one another, while others contradicting one another. They are all acceptable of course. Therefore, I recommend learning them – without thinking that with that your job is done!

Of course, this recommendation is not just for HR managers, but basically, when you study this particular field, where you are supposedly dealing with social aspects – things become clear.

How clear do they get?

As was stated in the *Introduction*, these are issues with long-term effects, which are difficult to quantify.

To illustrate this, here is a true story. There is a big company in Israel where, for years, their perspective was that there was no need for an HR department. How come? Because 'everyone is HR'.

To deal with these stigmas of 'a field that is a kind of an indulgence and not really a necessity', you need to be proficient not only in HR, but also in the understanding of other professions.

A good example of this occurred when we decided to cut back on overtime, resulting in the HR department having to go to every wing in the company to demand cutbacks. It all went well until we came to a certain unit where we were told that it was impossible for them to cut back. They had control rooms that required working in shifts, as well as daily professional and technical maintenance events that required the presence of employees for an indefinite amount of time.

The issue could have been closed right there, but we decided to do an in-depth examination. We investigated the job description, what it entails and what the function was in the field – to understand the principle and then see if, within these conditions and limitations, it was possible to preplan the overall picture more efficiently.

This is how we discovered that systematically work began there at 8am and ended at 5pm, but there were always malfunctions and delays that continued until seven in the evening. We suggested building a different kind of work plan. The suggestion was for one or two employees every day, to take turns arriving at 10am and staying until 7pm. Thus, the overtime would be covered. This was only one out of a few recommendations that was accepted after we examined what was really happening in the field.

"Too much agreement kills chat"
Eldridge Cleaver

Sometimes It Is a Stranger Who Understands!

To make our lives a little harder, once we have learned and understood the organization from different angles, including the financial aspect, there is another aspect I try to incorporate in the process and that is placing external devil's advocates wherever possible. I mainly try to bring them into working teams when dealing with a significant issue. This is an important factor, which shines a light in places of which you are not always aware. Everyone understands its importance, but they do not always insist – I recommend not letting up.

In strategic discussions in the business world, we try to incorporate external professionals, from the world of art, music or acting, simply because they are not trapped inside prejudice. So even if 20 irrelevant ideas are thrown into the air, maybe one hits the mark, and then the effort will be rewarded.

I have taken this principle one step further, using it when I put together working teams in a very specific niche. Take for example an organization in which I recognized that they had a big problem with recruitment. To compile think tanks in the matter, I requested that not only HR and recruitment experts participate, but also workers from the field, with the ability to get a much broader point of view. In order to refine and provide another angle, we invited internal customers as well as end-user customers. They definitely contributed in a way the team could not have.

By the way, we instilled the importance of dialogue and consultation with the internal customers within the level of the company, in all units. Employees learn how effective it is to match expectations and moreover – to include them in actual dilemmas. After all, you are always blind to your blind spots. The field has proven that this is the way to achieve better results.

To illustrate the principles of involving so-called 'strangers' in every area, I will bring a contemporary example – we are dealing now with the digitalizing and developing of possible worlds. Naturally, for such a task, we included people from the field of engineering,

IT, marketing and maybe even customers. We took it one step further and incorporated employees from the different worlds of content in the company, including financial and HR personnel. Aspects that are supposedly not their core line of business and precisely why they will come as *tabula rasa*.

Of course, in order to bring them up to date on the general context, preparation is required, mainly by whoever is leading the team. The relevant information needs to be presented – the topic, the background, and the environment – in order to allow them to really be focused on that particular world of content. Then, as mentioned, there is an increased chance of encountering ideas that I am not sure we would have heard otherwise.

Discretion Is the Name of the Game

During the mapping and assessment stages, especially in an unfamiliar organization, you are required to earn your professional place with the employees in general, and specifically in a complex way with the managers and VPs. It will not come out of the likes of – 'Pleased to meet you. I am here to advise you.' The classic situation, in which I believe and strive for, is to bring managers to the point in which they seek advice from you. This is something that always takes time because it happens only once they have learned that you are professional and trustworthy.

Discretion is the keyword here. Its importance cannot be overstated throughout the whole process and not just in the mapping process. If you are indiscreet, you will be burned pretty quickly and hard. I have already met HR personnel whose careers were wiped out due to their inability to keep things subtle.

A young manager asked me if I had ever had a dilemma regarding discretion – and the truth is – never. I never have. The moment that I am speaking with someone, and it becomes obvious to the both of us that the discussion is for our ears only, it stays that way. If something is said that I think is dramatic in its level of impact or harm, I always tell the person before I try to act on it or come up with indirect ways to resolve the issue that has arisen.

Let us take a case in which I am sitting with a VP who has an issue with the CEO. Obviously, I will not approach the CEO to tell them that their employee is complaining about the way they are being treated, but I will put it in the back of my mind until I find another way. An opportunity close enough to the issue always pops up, and so the issue can be brought to the table incidentally, and not from a personal place. Your gain is twofold – not only did you not reveal your source, but you also took care of the issue, or at least brought it up for discussion.

Obviously, there are situations that are more serious. One such time was a VP who consulted with me regarding a personal matter, seeking my opinion as to whether or not it was time to start looking for a position outside the organization. This is a highly sensitive matter, and my way of handling the situation is to try guiding them to speak to the CEO directly. I try to calm any apprehension, explaining that a conversation from a clean, genuine, and sharing place is the best way to go.

I also explain many times that there is no reason why

employees cannot share out aloud and in a direct manner that they are interested in pursuing a new professional path.

What will happen if employees share such information?

It is not as if they are going to get up and leave straight away, with the need to find an immediate replacement. On the other hand, many positive things can come out of such a discussion with the CEO. They may have a plan that will involve the employees in ideas of which they were unaware. In other words, in these situations, I always try for the direct connection.

This kind of discussion, in which a manager seeks your advice, will most probably not occur in your first few months in the organization, because it takes time to create strong infrastructures of trust and professional admiration. If you are not respected, then you will not be approached. However, discretion is what you are required to demonstrate from your first day in the job.

Employee Representatives Also Enjoy Successes

I recall another story, right at the beginning of my journey, which demonstrates additional necessary characteristics from a different direction. I entered a workplace, and after carrying out the mapping process, I wanted to share the results with the employee representatives as well. I gathered the entire HR team and all the representatives, and we gave an excellent presentation, explaining what we saw, what we did and what we recommend should be done. Just before I finished the presentation, all the employees got up and left.

The HR managers were shocked with the dramatic exit and said – "Okay, so there is no plan."

I replied – "Did you not understand that the plan has begun this very moment?"

Pointing at the door, they said – "But they are not with us!"

"They are not with us at this moment," I replied – "but if we will exhibit professionalism, faith on our part, determination and commitment to execute, together with personal examples and leadership – people will join us."

I explained to them what I believe to this day and that is – if things make sense, eventually, together with all the apprehension, fears, emotions, and past precipitations – people will connect, if only because they enjoy success.

Eat Your Hat! We began the process in the company, and at its completion, we held an outdoor event. After the event, we decided to do something fun to conclude. I invited the members of the committee to this event as well, and they came, I believe, out of curiosity. When they arrived, they picked up the vibe, and then after hearing the summary, one of the senior committee members stood up and courageously said in front of everyone – "I am forced to eat my hat. I did not fully comprehend what you had been talking about. I thought that it was all a show to accomplish other goals. I was wrong, and I am glad that HR insisted on continuing with the process, not giving up and recruiting us to it as well." From that moment, they basically took ownership of the project, which suited me fine. The organizational buzz that the process created in the end was completely unpredictable. The intensity was about the only thing that was hard to predict.

Of course, although I was confident and I knew what the road down the line looked like, there were concerns and difficult moments, but then it finally became clear to me that if you analyze, assess, and identify correctly, using the appropriate tools for treatment, and displaying them in the field – there is a good chance it will work. The buzz will follow suit!

"None of us is as smart as all of us"
Ken Blanchard

A Competition With No Losers!

One of the great projects we did was a digital project led by us. In my opinion, this project highlighted, in the best way possible, the will of employees and managers to work together when applied correctly.

In one of the companies, we decided as part of an internal-strategic organizational plan to have a contest for digital managerial initiatives – a common project in the hi-tech industry. The idea was to divide the employees and managers into working groups and each group chooses to deal with a topic that can promote the organizational or business aspect of the company. The goal was to change and design the organizational culture by harnessing all the employees to applicable tasks.

For this precise reason, we wanted to involve as many employees as possible from all levels of the organization, with the guiding assumption that this knowledge can actually be found in everyone. An additional assumption was that by doing this we would manage to join the internal forces to deal with company dilemmas and challenges, to find places for improvement and to do things differently.

For practical reasons, we pretty much allowed the participants to form into independent groups, but we made sure they came from different worlds of content and not all from the same field. Since it was a large organization with many possibilities, the employees largely integrated wherever they wanted. This way we also managed to recruit as many participants for the process as possible and we found a solution for each of the projects from every possible angle.

The participants got all the backup necessary from us, including the option to be accompanied professionally from external sources, and despite all this, to our delight, they mainly utilized internal forces. There were also projects where huge amounts of money were invested in their development to help get them off the ground. After all, these projects were chosen to eventually help the business, not just to be working theories on paper.

Among the topics this venture dealt with, there were projects for improving recruitment procedures, aiding in quicker identification of obstacles in bureaucratic procedures, presenting the organization's network status as a visual chart and creating a digital array to improve service and sales.

The project that won first place was called *Clients' EKG* and it dealt with the characterization, development, and assimilation of a tool for analysis in real time, allowing for the production of service, marketing and engineering insights.

What really amazed us was the level of responsiveness. All the employees and managers participated with enthusiasm and vigor. During one of the advanced stages, we held a marathon meeting lasting from morning to night, with all the managers from a level below the VPs, wandering amongst the groups, asking questions, learning the different topics, focusing, and helping.

This was a very significant happening, and the grand finale was a large conference where all the projects were presented to the entire company, including management. During this evening, prizes were awarded, intended to create an atmosphere of competition, which always adds to the occasion, but the most important thing, of course, was the way the process was handled.

Employees, used to being in the backrow, were provided with a stage. The fact that these projects actually happened, presented an opportunity for the employees to believe in open processes, together with the realization that these were not just empty promises made by management. Here their voices were heard; their professional opinions and capabilities were expressed and applied in the field.

At the end of the day, we had proof that the project actually worked and provided solutions, as well as results in additional circles. For example, it created a different dialogue – employees who had not met on a daily basis, and had barely spoke on the phone, were now grouping together in collaboration. It broke through boundaries and opened barriers between the employees.

We are all aware how sitting together, drinking coffee, and having meals brings people closer – creating an internal vibe and humor. The phone calls afterwards, during routine work, are different. It becomes much easier and more pleasant to cooperate with one another.

This whole process was unique because we knew to define, in advance, what we wanted to achieve and how to achieve it, from an organizational aspect and a business one. We involved the VPs in the project, emphasized which areas were important to us – and essentially engaged with the entire organization in a very long process, lasting almost a year. It is true that we did not invent the wheel here – but we built the venture correctly, thus it resonated for a long time. That, in itself, is greatness!

Throughout the years, I have instigated many initiatives in different companies, and I have come to the realization that from project to project my understanding has been enhanced. The experiences play to your benefit. You learn and understand where the important nuances are and how to pinpoint things. So, for me personally, the experience was not complicated and I was happy in any case to see that in addition to all the benefits we listed, the project combined all the development and HR teams. We were all together in the making – and this was definitely an added bonus!

CHAPTER 5

Tomorrow, Starting Today
Who Will the Next CEO Be?

"The future is not some place we are going to,
but one we are creating. The paths are not to be found,
but made, and the activity of making them, changes
both the maker and the destination"

John Schaar

**How will the workplace look in the future? What
will the admission requirements be? How flat will
organizations be in terms of hierarchy? Who will be
the future CEOs? Why will we need to prove that we
are worthy of being managers? How did Coronavirus
throw us into deep waters?**

When I was a young boy growing up in Haifa (a
city in Northern Israel) so many years ago, if we
wanted to find out what our future holds, we would buy
a *Bazooka* bubble gum and read the predictions on the
wrapper. 'By the age of 21, you will reach the moon' –
that was the prediction that excited us the most. Since
then, despite the promise, we have not really reached
the moon, but the 'tomorrow' is more intriguing than
ever and as the years have flown by, we have realized
that, without even being aware, the future has already
arrived.

At that same time in Haifa in the 1960s, the shelves
in my parent's house were packed full of encyclopedias,
and when we wanted to find out about something, we
burrowed in them. Whatever could not be found in the
encyclopedias simply did not exist. All the wisdom to be
found was on those shelves. Who would have believed

that one day all that information would be out in the open and available to everyone, the shelves would be emptied and the professions of the future would hinge on the ability to collect data and analyze it.

Theoretically, who would have thought that one would not have to learn anything, because everything to learn was in reach? Today, by surfing the Internet anyone with good comprehension and perception capabilities can learn as much about a certain field as a person with a college degree. So, we have been left with subjects still being studied at school, like literature and geography, that are obviously important and excellent for general knowledge, but if truth be told, once you have a minimal schooling background there is no problem to specialize and obtain all the information in every area from the Internet.

Once the information is accessible to learn a certain subject at a specific time, all that is needed is the ability to find and gather the information, which, as you are aware, is relatively easy, with even children knowing how to do it at the simplest level. The more complicated levels, which include data cuts and analysis – is a different story. Here we are dealing with, in my opinion, a future profession, which does not yet have a name or a university degree.

The Future Is Calling, India Is On the Line!
If we look around, we will see that even today we all take advantage of the available information in every area. Let us take, for example, technicians who have learned how to repair phones. They know their work – skilled

professionals, proficient in their profession in all its different shapes and sizes, and even though they are only required to repair equipment that they know very well, they constantly make sure to remain updated by checking online. They investigate any new equipment that comes to market, take apart its specifications and even build a curriculum for studying by themselves – for themselves. In other words, they use the available knowledge to sharpen and prepare themselves professionally for tomorrow.

In the world of HR, we do the same. As I write this book, we are facing a merger in the company where I work and so we need to understand more about what this means in terms of the integration of two organizational cultures. The topic has been discussed in a course, but now we are gathering all possible articles on the subject, to read and make notes for ourselves on the important points that can have an effect and optimize the process. With the professional tools provided by the general world of content, you can build a plan of action for yourself. This is collective wisdom at its best – wide knowledge, global research, companies who have gone through these procedures, where they have failed and where they have succeeded, results of the statistics etc.

So, it is obvious that the profession, which we are now calling 'the future' – is already here. We do not define it, but we are all already working in it without being aware.

Speaking of gathering information which is very much evolving today – I attended a very interesting lecture about the huge market developing in India where any sought-after information is available. All that is necessary is to send some computer geek the topic – and they will do the rest. Thousands of employees are employed mainly to collect facts about companies, businesses, and products. The fee is 15 dollars an hour, and eventually a folder containing files with all the information they could find is sent. And boy, do they find!

Job Admission, Search THIS for Me

The next step after collecting the information is the ability to analyze it – which in India is not so highly developed. This is where higher-level skills are required, but if this is your job on a daily basis and you are familiar with the world of content, then you already know how to analyze information, from which angles to check and what you are really looking for when deciphering it.

For the benefit of HR, it seems to me that more advanced stages will be needed in our criteria for job admissions. We will no longer look for basics. In other words, finishing a degree with distinction, although a good background check, is not enough for being suitable for the job. The most important attribute is in your ability to gather information and analyze the specific field in which you are meant to engage. This will be a major change. That is where the great specialization will come into play. I believe that in time the systems will become even more sophisticated, and will be able to collect accurate information, which today is still general. In parallel, there will probably be systems that can analyze some of this information. This is the direction.

Looking at the advanced organizations, especially in

the hi-tech industry, which determine the trends, we see that already today they are looking for the freaks and geeks. For them it is unimportant what the qualifications are of the candidates – they are only looking for the capabilities needed for production. They are less interested in certificates, academic degrees, or broader education. This is already happening now, and I think that this direction will expand.

Future Management, Business or Kibbutz?
In my opinion, future management is also expected to change. Even though the requirements have changed, we have still not adapted to them. Therefore, in most places traditional hierarchical management is still being preserved, even though everyone is talking the talk, aware of the fact that changes are coming. Yes, we say that employees need to be included, that we should take advantage of the collective wisdom, and we know that the brains are in the productive backbones – but how much of that is actually expressed in the field?

What are we doing about the new reality?

The answer is – too little.

From what I can see around me, there is definitely an improvement from the past; in some places, even significant improvement, but we are still not in the right place. As we have already mentioned – the hierarchy is still here, even though the younger generation no longer takes it into account.

Therefore, I also think that younger workers today, especially in the hi-tech industry, have a better chance of being future CEOs than their present counterparts, because the former are used to working in teams, to being part of a process and being attentive. Fellowship and collaborative thinking are definitely elements more suitable for the managers of the future.

On the other hand, it is precisely the fact that in forward-thinking companies there is no one taking responsibility and making decisions, that creates a fascinating contradiction. Because at the end of the day – a company is not a *kibbutz*.

Companies need the managerial backbone and decision-makers. But yes, nowadays managers cannot allow themselves to make too many decisions that annoy their employees. Even if employees are not speaking up and responding, that does not mean that things will be done as the manager intended, especially if employees do not relate to or are opposed to the guidelines.

How can this contradiction between the hierarchy and the management be solved? In my opinion, the future CEO will need to be a leader first and foremost – otherwise they will have no chance to lead an organization.

> *"Nothing we do is more important*
> *than hiring people. At the end of the day,*
> *you bet on people, not strategies"*
>
> **Lawrence Bossidy**

Periods of CEOs, The Future of the Soft Worlds

If we take a moment to examine the history of management in Israel and in the rest of the world, we will find different periods for the selection of CEOs skills. In the past, CEOs used to grow from the world of sales, then marketing; at a later stage, during our times, it was mainly the financial VPs who were chosen for promotion. Today we are indeed in a period where the CEOs understanding of business economics is more important.

I think that this trend is about to change. The capabilities, knowledge, and professionalism of the head of the organization will still carry weight, but the CEOs' success will not be measured by this, because these qualities ultimately are not the ones to count. Success and failure will be determined by the CEOs' ability to stimulate employees, by setting personal examples, by creating trust and the ability for tolerance, by gaining the employees' respect and thus ensuring their desire to listen and share. These are the important characteristics. Bottom line – a leader is required!

Indeed, it seems that this kind of leadership will become the main axis, and the face of the CEO will have to change, otherwise they will suffer the productive loss of their human capital. As we have already stated – all the other advantages are obsolete; the significant added value that remains is the employees themselves.

From this we can speculate that it is very possible that, in the future, the soft worlds of HR will have greater significance in the choice of who is eligible for the role of CEO. If I weigh up what the strengths and strong points the future CEO will require, it seems that HR personnel will have quite a few advantages.

After all, may it be tomorrow or the next day, we are talking about people. Even if there will be robots in certain places of work – people will still need to build them. And yes, the artificial intelligence and technological systems will advance and will make thinking easier, yet I cannot foresee a situation in which a robot will be able to replace all that is sensitive and humane. And in the end, these are the most powerful tools for management. Consider the fact that nowadays employees' actions are based mainly on their emotions, on the organization's connection to the environment and on the employees' connection to the company.

Internal Trainings, Locks Included

I also think that today we need to teach our employees data collection skills and analysis, on one level or another.

It may be that in the future separate tracks will be developed for those that excel at data collection and for anyone able to analyze proficiently. This is definitely a possibility. Not everyone needs to know how to do everything, but the standards must be set now to gain a clear advantage, in every area.

Another thing that has added value to any organization, and more and more training courses should be planned for it, is the ability to think out of the box. In my opinion, the need for it will grow with the impending changes.

Creativity, looking from a different angle, the perspective of the devil's advocate that we have already mentioned above – will become increasingly vital. Already today, a heavy weight has been placed on these angles in internal organizational studies.

Those who have attended conferences around the world have already seen the attempts to also expand this discourse in the world of managerial development, especially through games. This fieldwork aims at sharpening original inventive abilities that are largely built on work groups, challenges that require teamwork. As a side note, this also strengthens the direction of collaborative management we mentioned earlier.

The benefits are clear – even in the few professions in which creativity supposedly does not contribute in a direct manner, it expands one's outlook, creating an added value of a different perspective. Therefore, it sounds logical and essential to promote the topic of managerial development – but in reality – it is not so simple. A great mental and practical revolution is needed to implement it.

After all, from a very young age, we begin to develop patterns and build boundaries for ourselves. The educational system guides us into clearly defined squares, in which there is no room for creative thinking – just a pursuit after grades. The result of such a process is the creation of the existing employees – coming into the system with 700 locks and obstacles, finding it difficult to see beyond the end of their noses.

In my many meetings with managers, one of the main challenges I have encountered repeatedly is the lack of their ability to rise slightly above the system to see the big picture. It is very difficult to do this, since we are all so set in our ways.

I, too, who see myself as having a broad strategic out-

look, am aware of the unfortunate fact that I sin sometimes by forming barriers, and I am working on myself
to broaden my thinking and understanding.

So obviously, it is ideal to work on both fronts, and to
implement elements of thinking out of the box into the
educational systems, but these are not our responsibility. In places of work, solutions are needed today. If not,
once again we will find ourselves dealing with yesterday's problems.

FROM COMPUTER ENGINEERING
TO JAZZ

Professor David Passig, an expert on Future Studies and a consultant to international organizations, talks to us about the situation of HR and the skills of the future workers – an examination from another angle

Until today, HR considered their role to be more or less providing the skills the organization needs for its production process. No matter what line of production, the thought is always – 'We need to sort the people who have received training elsewhere and to continue teaching those we think are capable of passing the course.' The only indicator that is taken into account is the skills required by management, or the skills we think should be mastered.

In other words, the working assumption is that the production process requires a skillset that we need to find and empower for the company to move on to higher accomplishments. That is the paradigm. Could it be wrong? Absolutely!

The assumption is that there is someone who knows what the required skills for a particular production process are and this skillset can be defined, characterized.

Both these assumptions are being challenged in organizations and in intended production processes of the future. The assumption that someone 'knows' does not look so secure anymore, and one of the ways for organizations at the forefront to solve this issue is to create multidisciplinary groups that receive trainings that will be as broad as budgets will allow. In addition, to meet the challenge of not knowing the definitions of the required skills, many organizations are opening the ranks to larger and wider sets of performance capabilities, in the hope that those that fall in the net, will be of use to them. In this process, a huge fortune is lost.

If we look for a moment at the journey HR has taken, from when it was a small unit responsible for work admission forms, until today, where it is now part of the organizational development strategy, we find an impressive path, yet one that requires enormous resources. One of the reasons for this is that HR is in the midst of a historical period in which external organizations like universities and colleges, responsible for providing skillsets to the employees of the future, are also finding this difficult. Hence, HR are finding themselves taking on the job of the universities, which was not part of the definition of the unit's mission.

From here another paradigm is developing, predicting that there may be someone who knows better than the organizations what the future performance skillsets are – and that is the employees themselves. How come? Because they are more attentive, more in the field, and for them, it is a personal matter, so they follow the trends to provide themselves security. Therefore, employees' opinions regarding the required future skillsets need to be refined.

This is one aspect. The other aspect deals with the question – what skills will be required in the future?

It may turn out that the employees bring performance skills of which the organization is not aware. A graduate of computer engineering recruited into an organization could have other skills, unrelated, which may contribute to the organization. An example of this is if the graduate is a musician, and in a future production environment, the music could play a bigger part than engineering. Let us just say, for this matter, they play jazz. Jazz is the kind of music that is often improvised, has no notes and the music is played on the spur-of-the-moment, to form impressive patterns. This kind of skill is not written anywhere. If music is not on the agenda at that moment in time, it can definitely be incorporated into future production processes, once the organization becomes aware of its existence.

In other words, workers come to work today, especially from the new generation, with a broader education, diverse interests, and global minds. It is not like 30-40 years ago, when we finished university and went straight into a job. Today, people travel around the world, developing opinions, contacts, and values and have varied lines of work. No one today has only one field in which they are active, and the organization needs to map out these areas, which are unofficial, learning how to manifest them in the development and production processes. In fact, there is no system today that knows how to identify these hidden skills, nor does it motivate and reward the people expressing them in their work process.

Most employees have a great interest in the company, and a personal interest in continuing to develop their skills. Therefore, if we allow them to hone in as they see fit, and not according to what the organization thinks it needs, the rewards will be great. Skills no one thought relevant will come to the forefront, thanks to the employees' abilities.

The way things stand today, no employee can approach their manager and say something like – 'I want you to send me to a jazz course.' They would think the employee was crazy. Take my son for example – he has a degree in computers, spent a decade in the army and deals with encryption. So yes, he is excellent with encryptions, but what really interests him are computer games. Obviously, his workplace was unaware and thus no one asked – 'Hold on, how are your skill at developing computer games expressed in encryptions?'

In my opinion, an organization needs to know how to construct a model that hinges on a multitude of skills – and examples for such already exist in the world. I tried building such a model with a large company here in Israel. We tried creating, from within the organization, a market of skills. We offered different roles, requiring certain skills, and we asked who could fill these roles. A situation developed wherein employees could look for new positions with whatever skills they had. Then – whoever had 10 years of experience in encryption but sees that in the skills market the organization is looking for a computer games expert – benefits greatly, as will their place of work.

In the next stage, employees are given the opportunity to reveal the trainings they would like to undergo to advance themselves. Your advice can be – 'Listen, there is a market for existing skills, but there are other courses available that you can request to receive from us as part of training programs. Explain to us how it could contribute and maybe you could even teach your colleagues, or we could bring in such a course from external vendors.'

Organizations that are more open to defining skills, with the ability to use them and market them, are called 'open markets' and enjoy a higher percentage of success. Moreover, once they share the responsibility with their employees, making them partners – the level of satisfaction on both sides increases. A win-win situation is created!

Internal Organizational Communication, The World beyond the Desk

Another direction combining the technological developments with the ever-increasingly desire of employees to be involved, I find in the field of internal organization communication. In my estimation, it is going to occupy an increasingly central place down the road.

Basically, it is a topic which, in the past, never even existed in companies, and today it is flourishing in all. I still remember how, in my first years of working, the title 'Communication' was in fact 'Reporting to Employees'. After that, we created, as was acceptable during those times, an internal newsletter that was published every few months. This newsletter mainly included a message from the CEO with information about new activities in the welfare department. We called it 'Internal Organizational Communication', even though there was no communication at all, but more of a one-way message being conveyed from management to employees, in such irregularity, that sometimes between each newsletter half of the company could have been replaced.

Later the communication was improved and there were even initiatives at the level of the units to distribute a newsletter more frequently. At the *IEC* (Israeli Electrical Corporation), they even went so far as to broadcast internal news, which was kind of a breakaway development from the newsletter for employees.

Obviously, today it is a different world, and this topic is becoming more sophisticated. Firstly, there are platforms dedicated entirely to internal communications, and the focus has moved from the informative aspect to creating ongoing interaction with the employees.

There are still statements and messages that need to be conveyed, but they have become more sophisticated by creating the big picture – one that goes beyond the employee's desk and computer. As already mentioned, with a broader outlook the understanding and meaning of one's role creates a better connection.

I think that the communication needs to be taken one step further, with the employees from the field leading the way rather than, once again, the genius sitting at the top, presuming to know everything. Usually, that genius is **us** – HR. And surprisingly – we do not know everything!

Suggestions and Comments, What Is All that Noise?

Today, there are inner-organizational networks that act just like Facebook – they are open to all the employees to post and comment. This is very significant not only for the reasons we mentioned above, but also as a tool through which we can observe the underground currents in the organization.

I assume that very quickly these networks will use sophisticated analytical tools to identify such uproars. For example, I recently sat down with a company that is developing an algorithm able to identify and characterize basic points in your personality and in your prevailing mood according to the pictures you post on social networks. It looks amazing. They have checked it with over a few thousand people with an accuracy of over 90 percent. I believe that this kind of thing will very soon be integrated into the companies, to be used for identifying the organizational mood.

Today the internal pulse is measured through less sophisticated glasses, allowing one to see if someone is upset or when a serious problem has arisen. However, as already mentioned, I believe that tools that show trends, quantities, and distribution, and provide more accurate resolutions, will be implemented.

Just to calm the enthusiasm slightly and shoot ourselves in the foot once again, I want to revert to dealing with the problems that arise in the internal communication. By and large, even if there is no particular channel that allows feedback from employees, in most places they feel free to raise issues. The question is, as always, how are they received?

In this regard, allow me to remind you for a moment of the wooden box of 'Complaints and Suggestions for Improvements' that was once customary, and let me reveal to you that only when the lock became rusted, did we open the box! An improvement upon that was the 'Committee of Offers for Improvements', who would give a response to every complainant – 'Your offer is very nice; we will take it into consideration' – and that was the end of it.

We need to make sure not to once again fall into that trap, under the guise of advanced technology.

Family, Company, Sustainability. What Are Your Plans for the Summer?

Additional aspects of contemporary and future changes relate to the management of all our additional circles of needs – processes that are gaining momentum all the time. It turns out that employees do not come solo, even though it is convenient to think so at times. Obviously, the focus is always on the employees, but it is important to remember to take care of their additional needs.

The first circle being family of course, as it is obvious that if employees are unhappy at home, this will accompany them to work. Therefore, the obvious question here is – as a manager, how involved are you in what goes on? To what extent do you address problems that arise, and how flexible are you within today's very demanding framework?

This is true of all levels. For example, do you make sure that your employees go on their vacations, and do not stay late at work the whole week? Do you give any thought to the fact that during the summer, when there is no summer camp for the children, this can stress working parents out?

By the way, touching on the previous paragraph, doing something cosmetic can do wonders. So, for example, we organized a summer camp of our own in August, for the days when there were no other arrangements for the employees' children. Although it was only for three days, the effect was amazing, because once again, the moment you show your employee that you are aware of their problems and needs, even in their additional circles of needs, they appreciate it and show their gratitude very quickly.

The seemingly trivial fact that employees are not isolated from their lives requires a lot of investment with training managers specifically instilling the need to show sensitivity. As a manager who spends more time with your employees than your spouse, you need to learn to recognize a sour face, making sure it does not pass you by.

We are not talking about major revolutions here. Sometimes even one word (as trivial as it may sound) can make a difference. If your employee is not feeling well and goes home – did you give them a call? Did you text them? One is not always aware of the power behind a personal gesture, and sometimes it is not in one's character. To them I say – "This is important enough, so if you need to play the game – there is no choice – just play it."

"The statement by Ford that the people and the products come before profits was a wonderful thing"

Donald Petersen

No More 'Me', We Are All Together Now

The other circles that are important to address today, apart from the family, touches on the question of how the organization treats the public and the environment in general.

In other words, is this a company that preaches and practices social responsibility? This topic is taking up an increasingly serious spot in organizations' agendas.

People, mostly the younger ones, are demonstrating more and more concern and awareness to what is happening around them. Even if an employee, individually, does not really take any operative steps, they will still expect the company in which they work, to relate and be proactive. There is a generation growing in which the environment, wellness, pollution, social responsibility, and sustainability are definitely important.

The vast number of people with personal agendas and desires to have an impact in the field marks an almost inconceivable change, especially for someone like me, who remembers completely different incarnations. For example, even in the asbestos factories 20 years ago, when talks began about how it can cause cancer, there was no mass departure. People simply continued to work as always. This is unthinkable in today's terms.

Another example – in our organization there is great awareness of all these issues and among other things, a group was established that built up a wellness program which we encouraged and supported. As I have already mentioned, I have accumulated years of experience, so occasionally I think how absurd it is if one recalls the past. Then not only would an employee asking to create a running group have been thrown out the office, but employees would not even have dared to think that there was such an option.

Today people not only connect to organizations that relate to the environment, to society and to the community, but they also want to know what their company itself is manufacturing or selling. They no longer look through the narrow prism of 'only I am important', but are developing awareness and concerns, and are constantly exposed to the media – exposures that enhance and motivate this process more and more.

It is true that there are still companies that are not open to change, but it seems that this general direction is gaining great momentum. I see it not just in the broader environmental – social context, but also in the employees' desires to have an impact from inside.

Obviously, this does not necessarily have to be about contributions and monetary donations given directly to the community. Opportunities can also be made for employees to contribute to society through the company. This is twofold – employees are content and are aware of the company's commitment as well.

Let Us Plant a Tree Just for the Record

In all the previously-mentioned fields, there are companies choosing to be called 'green companies' but it is just for outward impressions. However, there are companies that really do act. I still feel that there are organizations announcing what they are doing, but it is often more for the record, and less from a place of real connection and actual understanding of the meaning of contributing.

After all, this falls under 'soft areas' – difficult to see and measure. What is more, this section requires large investments and a great passion.

The topic is important to all. Everyone understands just how important this is, but the question is, as always, what to do with this understanding. Some plant a tree in a forest. That is great; I am not dismissing that. However, activities like these seem more of a 'cover up' to me, because they are easy and convenient and do not require major efforts. In contrast, there are companies that genuinely reflect contributing in their perception, even their business perception. And this is where you can find really decent projects.

I once judged a competition, held between organizations, which dealt with social projects, because I wanted to be exposed to as many projects of community contributions as possible. What was common to them all was the understanding that one needs to give back, and that giving back, also helps the employees, because participating in such projects is rewarding in itself.

I was a witness to many admirable actions there. One such example was *Israel Aerospace Industries*. Engineers with phenomenal capabilities to solve technical issues were chosen to help people with all kinds of disabilities – and they created real solutions. This is obviously amazing from the human aspect and admirable thanks to the caring, creativity, investment, and the connection between the people there. When you happen upon such a thing, you think to yourself – "I made one person smile, what more do I need?"

Go Recreate the Excitement!

Here is a short story that proved to me up-close how rewarding contribution can be. A few years ago, in one of the companies I was working at, we had an employee who lived in a remote settlement, and we were not so sure what was going on with him. There seemed to be a feeling of distress surrounding him, but we could not manage to put our finger on it. The HR manager suggested we go and pay him a visit at his home to see what his situation was, but he evaded us time and again, until we included his friends from his department, and told him that we were all coming together to visit.

When we arrived there, we were all shocked and brought to tears by what we saw. The house was destroyed, dismantled with no windows, no running water, no furniture, and a rundown refrigerator.

We asked him why had he not said anything – it turned out that he was too ashamed.

Immediately, dozens of workers signed up for the mission and we bought all the materials. In just a few days, we rearranged the whole house for him. In the end, it was unclear who was more excited – the employee himself or all the volunteers. We were all vividly exposed to the unimaginable power of giving. This feeling cannot be recreated by any monetary reward, desserts in the dining room or fancy offices.

By the way, to illustrate just how enthusiastic and fulfilled this made the volunteers feel – they immediately began looking for other places in need of help afterwards, and we, of course, were completely behind the matter.

How Many Calories Burn on Stairs?

In truth, in almost every HR conference around the world, the topic of social responsibility arises. Obviously, people begin to inquire about the environment and society before they begin to work for a company. And there is a good reason for that – if, as an employer, you ignore the above, this testifies to you personally – so thank you very much, but there are other employers.

These issues are examined in the company I work for today from every aspect. For example, we have changed the entire menu in the dining room. There is now a large choice of vegetables and healthy food, and we have launched 'Meatless Monday'. Speaking about food – we have just begun a nice project of a recipe competition, where the winning recipe is prepared in the kitchen and its owner serves it from a special stand.

Also, we offer yoga classes in the organization, before and after work, together with many activities of all kinds of sporting groups, which we encourage. We even illuminated and marked the staircases in such a way that if one wants to use them for fitness purposes, it shows how many calories one burns up using the stairs.

"Don't judge each day by the harvest you reap but by the seeds that you plant"

Robert Louis Stevenson

A LITTLE SELFISHNESS
CAN HELP

Ayelet Gneezy, a professor at the Rady School of Management in San Diego (UCSD), who specializes and consults companies in issues relating to consumer behavior, marketing, and PR, conveys what we get out of charitable giving and investigates the correct way to do it

Every year, in October, *Microsoft* announces the month of giving. This is not a new trend, but a tradition going back to 1983. During this month, every employee is entitled to choose a social target to raise donations. It can be for the disabled, for high-risk children, society preservation or any other social area. In any case, the employees are invited to use all the company's means and facilities, even during working hours, to raise donations from friends, family members and colleagues for the organization of their choosing.

In addition, to support the employees *Microsoft* chips in. For example, if you manage to raise a certain amount of money, the company will match the amount at different levels. Let us say, you raised 100 dollars, the company will donate another 100. If 500 dollars is collected, they will double the amount − 1,000 dollars. The amounts change all the time. But what is important and wonderful here, of course, is the principle.

Firstly, you are passing the reins to the employees, and at the same time, letting them know something significant – we, as the company employing you, really care about what you care about. This message is amplified with every move that costs the company money, without immediate turnover.

This is one of the best examples, in my opinion, of connecting between a social target and a managerial target, because the concept behind it is an unambiguous statement – we are taking care of the environment and the community, but we will not tell you where to give, because we understand that everyone's heart may be in a different place.

Academic research has also proven how effective and correct this method is, because it embodies so many things. First of all, it shows how the company's commitment is genuinely across-the-board, because allowing employees to use company offices, technology, time and space for a month to raise money, is not something trivial. Second, as mentioned, the project allows the employees the opportunity to express their own values.

We have already mentioned in this book that, nowadays, employers cannot just hand out instructions to their employees, and this goes to helping the community and social involvement as well. The freedom of choice – provided in the above example – makes employees feel like partners. I assume that if *Microsoft* has been continuing with the project since 1983, there must be great importance attached to it judging by employee satisfaction. By the way, it is appropriate to also include this whole topic under the important umbrella of 'Communication in the Workplace', the significance of which cannot be overstated. And the impact organizational culture has on employees staying in the system and their feelings of satisfaction has already been proven.

The Summer Camp Effect Y+3

I really like the example of the summer camps described in this chapter, because I think there is something especially wonderful here, even though some may relate to the gesture in a cynical way. I see it like this – it is more important for the employees to know that their problems had been realized and there was concern to solve it, than actually solving it. Even if you are unable to find a solution, but make a relatively small gesture, you have at least made them feel that they are appreciated. They exist in your eyes.

This mini-summer camp example can be examined through research done in psychology, which tells about the different norms between the social connection and the monetary connection – i.e., Communal Relationship and Exchange Relationship.

In a nutshell, it goes like this – the communal relationship actually defines a friendly relationship, say between you and me. If you bought me a cup of coffee one day, I do not need to rush to pay you back immediately or tomorrow. There is no keeping score between us. However, if we are in an exchange relationship – after you have bought me a cup of coffee, I will feel obliged to pay you back straight away.

In most cases, the exchange relationship characterizes the relationship we have with our bank or our children's kindergarten teacher. The concept being that if you give something, you get something back. There are no open debts – everything is very clear. Meaning – *quid pro quo*. You give – you get!

Basically, between employees and management, there is a relationship of exchange. Employees give of their knowledge, time and effort and get a salary in return. The norms dictating this relationship are clear and businesslike. I think that in the case of the summer camps, employees were surprised – a three-day, two-day, or even half an hour summer camp, conveyed the message to the employees that management were deviating from the norms that define the relationship, changing the way they see the employees.

In other words, the relationship defines that if you do X, then I give Y, and now in this same relationship, you are doing X and I am giving you Y+3 and it is not as if I am giving more of the same, but am going the extra mile. We did not turn a friendship into a business relationship, but we added a personal and considerate dimension to our business relationships. Bingo!

Are You Keeping Up? Another angle that is important to me, is the issue of consistency. For example, if the company claims to care about the environment and therefore asks employees to turn off the lights and air-conditioning at the end of the day, then it is important that this concern for the environment is visible in other areas as well. It can be reflected in the fact that there are recycling bins, in the type of products the company buys and even the vehicle the CEO drives.

I think that if this is not the case, i.e. on one hand you are telling me as an employee to save costs, and on the other hand, you drive a jeep that consumes a lot of gas – you are on the right track to harm your credibility and the seriousness of your intentions. You say one thing but do another – for your own consideration. This is a point worth taking into account!

> *"Setting an example is not the main means of influencing others, it is the only means"*
>
> **Albert Einstein**

Can I Please Fix Your House?

I would also like to relate to the academic explanation regarding giving, in general, using the example of the employee and the help with his house. We saw that once the volunteers had finished renovating his house, they went on to other projects.

Why was that, actually?

In the beginning of the 1990s', a behaviorist economist by the name of James Andreoni coined the term 'Warm Glow', which claims that no giving is completely altruistic.

It works like this – when you do something nice for someone – donate money, help someone across the street, or, the example mentioned earlier – help fix a ruined house – given the fact that you are helping someone, which is very altruistic, it also contains a slight element of selfishness. It comes from the fact that such an act makes you feel good about yourself. So, in this context, we can say that the employees continued to work on additional projects to help and make a change, because they realized that it made them feel good. By the way, this is not a feeling you will get if you give because you were told to give, or because you know that you are expected to – as what happens in many workplaces.

In *Timberland*, for example, they have a program similar to that of the employee and his house, yet it is more regular and orderly, where employees can volunteer for one day a month, at the company's expense. Groups of employees collaborate to do renovations, paint fences, structures etc., and again – it is all of the employees' choosing.

This is the place to clarify that if volunteering is part of the framework of your job and it makes you feel good about yourself, part of that feeling should be linked back, consciously, or unconsciously, to the company. And here we have gained a little something worthwhile along the way!

"The key to successful leadership today
is influence, not authority"

Ken Blanchard

A POINT TO CONSIDER

WHO SHOULD REALLY BE ENTITLED TO MANAGE?

A key question that I would like to raise in conclusion is – who is entitled to be appointed manager? Today when an employee, who is an excellent and successful professional and brings great results, is promoted to manager – it makes one wonder if all of the above has earned them the privilege to lead people

Considering the changes in the workplace, which we have talked about, I believe that this will be the next question employees ask out aloud. At the heart of the matter is the fact that management has basic technical dimensions, but what happens beyond those? We all know that the position requires a degree, experience, and knowledge. That is it. I have never seen a wanted ad looking for someone who is also a decent human being.

We have mentioned here already that in hi-tech companies, the managerial hierarchy is becoming flatter and flatter and I believe that the entire business world is going in that direction. The facts are written in the field – a lot more knowledge that does not necessarily have to do with a formal education, is available to all employees, at all levels, in all ranks. As a result, employees are a lot more opinionated, more aware of their rights and less inclined to be manipulated and treated with disrespect.

The era of – 'They are right because they are managers' – is over!

In my opinion, the process will continue to escalate and rise to the surface, requiring serious deliberation – is it not essential to include interpersonal capabilities among all the other managerial skills?

An existing graph clearly shows that the lower your emotional intelligence is, the more you are unable to bring out the most in people – the chances of you being unsuccessful are higher.

It is no secret that, when high-functional employees leave their jobs, they are not quitting the company, but are leaving the people who work there – mainly their direct managers. A lot of this stems from the mistranslation we mentioned, from managers getting confused between inner strength and force. This is a very tricky situation, and it is influenced by what you, as the manager, convey outwardly. A forceful boss radiates a message that sabotages the goal, compared to managers with inner strength, who set personal examples, using their professional capabilities and tolerance. Having true power obviates the need to fight all the time and to pull rank.

I think that these procedures are clear to everyone – there is no one who will disagree, but in practice, it is obvious that this continues. Repeatedly, I find myself troubled by my discussions with managers, no matter on what level, who complain about their managers. After a little digging, I find that those who complain are behaving in the same way towards their subordinates. In most cases, this occurs without anyone paying attention and without a drop of awareness. I have not heard many managers say – 'I think that I am too forceful' or 'I may not be attentive enough to my employees.'

On the other hand, I constantly hear complaints to the tune of – 'My manager does not listen to me'; 'My manager does not see me'; 'My manager speaks to me disrespectfully.' The bickering is always aimed towards the upper levels. This sets out clearly what managing should look like, which we have not properly internalized, preferring to sweep it under the rug and turn a blind eye.

This is exactly where, in my opinion, the field should come in. Change will not come from the management level, but from below. And the sooner managers will learn to prepare the groundwork, to form the right platform – the less it will catch them by surprise. Therefore, I say, let us be able to look ourselves in the eye, because there is no doubt that tomorrow someone will ask how we earned the right to lead people.

"Change is the law of life. And those who look only to the past or present are certain to miss the future."

John F. Kennedy

An Additional Word for the End:

The book began with a description of working relationships during the Coronavirus, but the truth is that I was already towards the end of the book, when the virus burst into our lives. The drama and revolution caused by it (including effects still not measurable) have forced us to reexamine almost every aspect in our personal and professional lives. Therefore, it is logical that, in light of Coronavirus, I am constantly reexamining the concepts, principles and model presented here.

In the face of this new reality, the message that is important for me to convey is – that at the end of the day what will decide from now on are our values as human beings, as a society, as a community – is it still relevant?

In my humble opinion, and according to my experience during this period – more than ever!

MY COMPASS

FROM WORKING RELATIONSHIPS TO RELATIONSHIPS THAT WORK

DO NOT MANAGE — LEAD!

DO NOT ACT WITH FORCE —
ACT WITH INNER STRENGTH!

SPEAK LESS — LISTEN MORE!

LET GO OF YOUR EGO — ALLOW OTHERS!

DO NOT ACT ONLY FROM YOUR MIND —
USE YOUR EMOTIONS AND LOGIC!

DO NOT CRITICIZE — GUIDE!

DO NOT WAIT — INITIATE!

DO NOT WITHHOLD INFORMATION —
DEMONSTRATE TRANSPARENCY!

"Far better it is to dare mighty things, to win glorious triumphs, even though checkered by failure, than to take rank with those poor spirits who neither enjoy much nor suffer much, because they live in the gray twilight that knows neither victory nor defeat"
Theodore Roosevelt 1899

REFERENCES

CHAPTER 1
Management and Leadership

- Edersheim Haas, Elizabeth (2007). *The Definitive Drucker: Challenges for Tomorrow's Executives -- Final Advice from the Father of Modern Management. Chapter 5: People and Knowledge*. McGraw Hill.
- Collins, Jim (2001). *From Good to Great. Chapter 2: Level 5 Leadership*. Random House.
- Collins, Jim (2001). *From Good to Great. Chapter 6: Level 5 A Culture of Discipline*. Random House.
- Drucker, P. (2004). *What Makes an Effective Executive*. Harvard Business Review, 82(6), 59-63.

HR Development

- Meshoulam, Ilan & Harpaz, Itzhak (2015). *Human Resource Management – The Strategic Approach. Chapter 1: The Essence of Human Resource Management*. Haifa, University of Haifa.

Change Management

- Levy, Amir (2000). *Mastering Organizational Change: Theory & Practice*. Tel Aviv: Tcherikover.
- Levy, Amir (2007). *Management & Leadership, Change & Innovation*. Tel Aviv: Rimonim.
- Fox, Shaul (1998). *The Psychology of Resistance to Change*. Ramat Gan: Bar Ilan.
- Kotter, John (1996). *Leading Change*. Harvard Business Review Press.
- Kotter, John (2008). *A Sense of Urgency*. Harvard Business Review Press.
- Kotter, John (1995). *Leading Change: Why Transformation Efforts Fail*. Harvard Business Review, March-April, 56-67.
- Kotter, John (2014). *Accelerate: Building Strategic Agility for a Faster-Moving World*. Harvard Business Review Press.

Coronavirus and Working in Organizations

- Cohen, Nirit (08.10.2020). *Working from Home Efficiency Indices: Forget About Tracking Work Hours.* Globes.
- Cohen, Nirit (31.10.2020). *Together yet Apart: How will Offices Look around the World Post-Covid.* Globes.
- Cohen, Nirit (18.11.2020). *There is No Going Back Once You Have Seen Your Employees in Sweats.* Globes.

Call Centers Management - Challenges in Recruitment & Retention

- Novella R. J. (2020). *Call Center Management Strategies to Increase Job Satisfaction and Reduce Employee Turnover.* Walden University.

Emotional Intelligence in Management

- Goldman D. and R. Boyatzis (2008). *Social Intelligence and the Biology of Leadership.* Harvard Business Review Press.
- Goldman D. (2019). *The Emotionally Intelligent Leader.* Harvard Business Review Press.
- Samuel, Yitzhak (1990). *Organizations: Characteristics, Structures, Processes. Chapter 11: Organizational Culture.* Haifa: University of Haifa/Zmora-Bitan.
- Drucker, Peter (2006). *The Practice of Management. Chapter 13: The Spirit of an Organization.* Harper Business.

Career & Management Patterns in the Field of HR Management

- Meshoulam, Ilan & Harpaz, Itzhak (2015). *Human Resource Management – The Strategic Approach. Chapter 1: The Job Requirements of Human Resource Management.* Haifa, University of Haifa.
- Meshoulam, Ilan & Harpaz, Itzhak (2015). *Human Resource Management – The Strategic Approach. Chapter 4: The Role of the Human Resource System in Managing the Organizational Culture.* Haifa, University of Haifa.

- Meshoulam, Ilan & Harpaz, Itzhak (2015). *Human Resource Management – The Strategic Approach. Chapter 16: The Professional Requirements from Human Resource Personnel.* Haifa, University of Haifa

Roundtables & Open Doors
- Bitner, Dotan (2018). *The Blog: Is Anybody Here Doing Roundtables in the Organization?*
- Kane, Hadar (28.06.09). *The Way to the Employee's Heart is Through the Boss's Room.* Globes.

CHAPTER 2
Labor Relations & Trade Unions
- Levy, Shelly (2006). *The Right of Association in Israel.* Department of Information & Research. Submitted to the Labor, Welfare and Health Committee.
- Fisher, Eran (2019). *Discourse of Hi Tech Workers in Israel 2014-2018.* Israeli Sociology, Workbook 2, 10.

Active Listening as an Assessment Tool
- Whitworth, Laura, Kimsey-House, Henry & Sandahl, Phillip (1998). *Co-Active Coaching. Chapter 2: Co-Active Coaching Skills – Listening.* Nicholas Brealey Publishing.

Strategic-Organizational Assessment
- Bohlander G. W. et al. (2001). *Managing Human Resources 12th Edition. Chapter 4: Human Resources Planning and Recruitment.* South-Western/Thomson Learning.
- Snell S., Morris S. and Bohlander G. W. (2015). *Managing Human Resources 17th Edition. Part 1: Strategy and Human Resources Planning.* Cengage Learning.

Outdoor Events as an Assessment & Organizational Development Tool
- Patching K. (1999). *Management and Organization Development: Beyond Arrows, Boxes and Circles.* Macmillan Press.

- Reid M. Et al (2004). *Human Resource Development: Beyond Training Interventions.* CIPD House Cromwell Press.

Feedback Discussions

- Posthuma, R.A. and Campion, M.A. (2008). *Twenty Best Practices for Just Employee Performance Rreviews. Compensation and Benefits Review, Vol. 40 (1), January/February. Pp. 47-55.*

Talent Development and Pipeline Leadership

- Snell S. and Morris S. (2016). *Managing Human Resources 12th Edition. Part 3: Developing Effectiveness in Human Resources.* Cengage.

Management and Ego

- Cohen, Anat (10.08.2005). *It Is Beneath Me – The Road to Success in Business Requires Knowing When to Let Go of Your Ego.* Globes.

Organizational Synergy and Effectiveness

- Peters, Thomas J. & Waterman, Robert H. (1984). *In Search of Excellence. Part 3 - Simultaneous Loose–Tight Properties.* HarperCollins Publishers Inc.

CHAPTER 3
Working Relationships in the Role of HR

- Nathanson, Roby & Gazala, Itamar (2016). *Israeli Guide for Co-Determination and Corporate Sustainability.* Macro Center for Political Economics & The Hans Böckler Foundation.
- Meshoulam, Ilan & Harpaz, Itzhak (2015). *Human Resource Management – The Strategic Approach. Chapter 5: New Trends in Human Resource Management.* Haifa, University of Haifa.

Measuring RoI in the Field of HR

- Meshoulam, Ilan & Harpaz, Itzhak (2015). *Human Resource Management – The Strategic Approach. Chapter 2:*

The Strategical Approach to Human Resource Management. Haifa, University of Haifa.
- Gupta A.D (2020). *Strategic Human Resource Management: Formulating and Implementing HR Strategies for a Competitive Advantage. Chapter 6: Improving Business Performance through Strategic HRM.* Routledge NY.

Motivating Employees and Organizations
- Peters, Thomas J. & Waterman, Robert H. (1984). *In Search of Excellence. Part 1 – A Bias for Action.* HarperCollins Publishers Inc.
- Nicholson, N. (2003). *How to Motivate your Problem People. Harvard Business Review, 81 (1), 56-65.*

Organizational Synergy
- Adizes, Ichak (2010). *Mastering Change.* IDF Publishing Systems Ministry of Defense.

CHAPTER 4

Business Organizational Strategy
- Collins, Jim & Porras, Jerry (1994). *Built to Last: Successful Habits of Visionary Companies (Good to Great, 2).* Harper Business.
- Somekh, Smadar & Kadry, Halad (2017). *The Future of the Working World: Overview of Major Trends.* Myers – JDC – Brookdale.
- Williams, S. (2016). *Future Skills: Update and Literature Review.* The Joyce Foundation.

Internal Organizational Communication
- Samuel, Yitzhak (1990). *Organizations: Characteristics, Structures, Processes. Chapter 6: Communication and Science.* Haifa: University of Haifa/Zmora-Bitan.

Strategic Social Responsibility
- Porter, M. E., & Kramer, M. R. (2006). *Strategy and Society: The Link between Competitive Advantage and Corporate*

Social Responsibility. Harvard Business Review, 84(12), 78-92.

- Yuan, W., Bao, Y., & Verbeke, A. (2011). *Integrating CSR Initiatives in Business: An Organizing Framework.* Journal of Business Ethics, 101(1), 75-92.

Social Contribution in an Organization (Prof. Gneezy)

- Andreoni, J. (1989). *Giving with Impure Altruism: Applications to Charity and Ricardian Equivalence.* Journal of Political Economy, 97 (6), 1447-1458.
- Andreoni, J. (1990). *Impure Altruism and Donations to Public Goods: A Theory of Warm-Glow Giving.* The Economic Journal, 100 (401), 464-477.
- Austin, James E. and Leonard, Herman B. (2004). *Timberland: Commerce and Justice.* Harvard Business School, Case 305-200.

Made in United States
North Haven, CT
06 January 2024

46876079R00127